"How do you respond when your life is shattered and hundreds of churches are destroyed? *Serving God Under Siege* invites you into a courageous journey of radical love that will strengthen your faith. You will be inspired and equipped to stand boldly with the persecuted, serve your community with compassion, and embrace Holy Spirit creativity to bring transformation. Filled with harrowing stories and an even more powerful God, *Serving God Under Siege* is not just a book; it's a call to action that will leave a lasting impact."

—ELIJAH M. BROWN, General Secretary and CEO, Baptist World Alliance

"Valentyn Syniy's account of his escape from Kherson with his family, his constant anxiety for his church and seminary, is incredibly moving. The story vividly portrays the devastation wrought by the Russian army in eastern Ukraine and its impact on Ukrainian churches. It is an arresting narrative—fast-paced, gripping, and hard to put down. The book illuminates important realities: the personal fear and tragedy of a refugee, the humanitarian crisis, the struggles of church leaders amidst the invasion, and a man's love for his church, country, family, and home."

—MICHAEL F. BIRD, deputy principal of Ridley College

"I can't remember the last time I read a book in one sitting—until now. *Serving God Under Siege* gripped me from the first chapter to the end. In this powerful and honest account, Valentyn Syniy offers a deeply personal account of the first months of the Russian invasion of Ukraine. Through his eyes, we witness the heartache, dilemmas, ministry challenges, and life lessons forged in the crucible of suffering engulfing his nation. Every Christian should read this book—not only to see beyond the headlines, but to understand how to stand faithfully with our brothers and sisters in Ukraine."

—ROBIN HARRIS, chair of the Center for Excellence in World Arts, Dallas International University

"As my own father came from his beloved Ukraine; and as a number of our Ukrainian relatives were war refugees for whom my extended family raised support; and as my wife and I visited Ukraine during wartime, spoke with our Ukrainian friends and relatives, and witnessed some of the devastation wrought by the Russian army, this powerful story by Valentyn Syniy struck home in a singular way. His book describes the impact of the Russian invasion of Ukraine on his own family and his nation: the horrors and atrocities, the displacement and disorientation of refugees, but also the hope of the gospel in the midst of the rubble. This deeply personal war autobiography exhibits courageous Christian leadership and Spirit-filled community in the face of loss, anger, confusion, and moral struggle."

—PAUL COPAN, Pledger Family Chair of Philosophy and Ethics, Palm Beach Atlantic University

"Honest. Personal. Deeply moving. These are words that come to mind when (not if) one reads Valentyn Syniy's eyewitness account of Russia's invasion of Ukraine. The book goes beyond the lead story of the evening news, into the hearts and minds of Syniy and the Tavriski Christian Institute community. This book is a page-turner, one you will find difficult to put down."

—MARK SCOTT, professor emeritus of preaching and New Testament at Ozark Christian College and Lincoln Seminary

"War in Congo claimed many lives and displaced my wife and her family for eighteen months. Syniy's book reveals the speed at which the normalcy of peace can be shattered by the horrors of war and displacement, even in a comparatively economically advanced setting like Ukraine, in Europe. This book also testifies to the spirit of those who, in Christ, find and create hope for the future from the remains of the past."

—CRAIG S. KEENER, F. M. and Ada Thompson Professor of Biblical Studies, Asbury Theological Seminary

Serving God Under Siege

—

HOW WAR TRANSFORMED A UKRAINIAN COMMUNITY

—

Valentyn Syniy

William B. Eerdmans Publishing Company
Grand Rapids, Michigan

Wm. B. Eerdmans Publishing Co.
2006 44th Street SE, Grand Rapids, MI 49508
www.eerdmans.com

Published 2025
Printed in the United States of America

Chapter opening illustrations by Maryna Polegenko

31 30 29 28 27 26 25 1 2 3 4 5 6 7

ISBN 978-0-8028-8569-2

Library of Congress Cataloging-in-Publication Data

A catalog record for this book is available from the Library of Congress.

Contents

Preface to the English-Language Edition

Dear readers,

It is a great honor for me to introduce this book to English-speaking readers.

I was born in Ukraine during the Communist regime in the USSR. As a member of a Baptist family, I grew up hearing that evangelical Christians were a "sect," second-class citizens. We were told that we would not be allowed to go to university, get an education, or travel abroad. However, thirty years have passed, and God has given me the opportunity to have my book translated for American readers—something that was impossible to even dream of under the Communist dictatorship.

This book you are holding in your hands tells the story of a man who experienced internal migration in his own country after Russia launched a full-scale invasion of Ukraine. I realize that the war we are experiencing today is far from the first in human history and, unfortunately, probably will not be the last.

The book was conceived as an honest account of what it is like to be displaced during a war in the modern world, very often a world of lonely people. This is the view of an ordinary person, a displaced person, who was not a soldier but served as a pastor of a church and was the president of a seminary in the south of Ukraine. In the Ukrainian edition, this book is called *The Man Whose Home Was Stolen: The Fight for Freedom*. For me, the main tragedy of the war was the loss of my home and the destruction of the seminary campus, where I have served as rector for nineteen years.

When I was writing this book, I asked myself: Why am I so hurt by the loss of society, the destroyed city and community in which I grew up, but not so sorry for the brick walls of my home? I found the answer in the fact that in our language there are two concepts of home. Home as a physical place—a building, a plot of land, property. And home as a place of communication, where a person meets with God and with other people, like in the Garden of Eden. I realized that the war destroyed this second concept of home—home as a place of communication and unity.

I understand that it can be difficult to convey these cultural and spiritual concepts to another audience. That is why I supported the editorial board's advice to change the title of the book in English to *Serving God Under Siege: How War Transformed a Ukrainian Community*. This title more clearly conveys the meaning of the book for a wider audience.

Also, let me draw your attention to the illustrations in the book. For me, this book is a confession of an adult man, a kind of prayer at the altar. And since confession is often sad, I discussed with the illustrator the idea of black-and-white images. However, in order to convey hope, I asked that each illustration contain a color element, symbolizing a ray of light and faith in the best.

The book's illustrator is a native of Kherson, like me. She also experienced emigration, moving to Germany, while I remained in Ukraine. That is why I chose her for this work—she perfectly understands the emotions that permeate my story.

I realize that the realities described in the book may differ from your experience. However, I hope that this honest conversation will help anyone who is looking for a way to their home—a home where you are accepted and where you can be yourself. I also think that this book can help a person who is experiencing the wounds from the losses we face in life.

The war taught me to value people. People are usually much more fragile, and their recovery much more difficult, than we sometimes think. I sincerely hope that this book will inspire you to value the people around you.

Dear readers, I am very grateful that you picked up this book. It is a great comfort and encouragement to me to know that my confession has found a response.

With blessings,
forgiven sinner, traveler,
and happy husband
Valentyn

Prologue

Everything was the same as he had remembered it and yet very slightly changed, as if the place and he had grown older at different rates.

—Graham Greene, *The Tenth Man*

November is the time of the first frost in Kherson. I remembered it after failing to open the lock of the gate to my house. That used to happen once a year. Usually, I would oil the lock before the cold weather came. If I failed to do that, the lock would not work properly, "reminding" me of the annual ritual. I did not notice the light frost outside while our gray Volkswagen Crafter, with its "Volunteer" sign at the front window, was making its way cautiously along familiar streets.

"Are you cold?" asked my brother Stas, leaving the driver's seat to help me with the lock.

"And there is no oil handy," I said.

The gate finally gave way. I entered a yard littered and overgrown with weeds. In some places they had even raised the tiles. Behind me, Stas was playing with the lock, trying to get it to work properly, while saying, "Frozen, frozen, frozen." At that moment, it seemed to me that everything was frozen: time, life, nature. Frozen from that February morning when my family and I left our home. Nine months earlier.

Chapter 1

Smell of War

WAR IS DETESTABLE. NO MATTER WHICH SIDE wins and resumes the blossom of life, life becomes a desolate landscape. Attributes of war bring destruction to the world. Its essence is a menace to well-being. All its attributes—smell, taste, sight, touch—are the tentacles of death that seek to take away, to break, to kill.

War has a peculiar smell. Many will agree with that. Some are immediately reminded of movie scenes depicting the smoke and heavy fumes of the fires caused by shelling. Those who have experienced war remember the smell of the battles: the aroma of freshly bombed soil, the stench of burnt flesh or dead bodies that cause vomiting. The odor is an integral part of war. But smell is also a warning sign. Think of a smoldering firebrand. Before you see it, you can smell it, and then the fire comes. It is the same with the stench of war, which began on February 24, 2022. We could smell it long before the glow of battles lit up our cozy city of Kherson.

The stench of war has been soaring all over Ukraine for eight years, beginning with the annexation of the Crimea and the invasion of "polite green men" into Donbas. Everything that was happening then seemed alarming, making one believe that the whole country would be on fire soon. But each time, the threat receded and the smoke evaporated. Or could we have been simply deceiving ourselves, holding to a clearly unjustified hope? Believing that our "neighbor" would not abandon reason and humanness completely. As humans, we just wanted peace. But by the end of 2021, a persistent "smell" of war was supplemented by quite visible contours of militarist-front smoke. War rhetoric accelerated. Extensive drills were taking place all along the Ukrainian border. One wicked provocation followed another. Every day there would be some incident that made the eyes burn because of acrid smoke. It was becoming more and more difficult to live and plan under such circumstances.

It was not easy for me, as the president of Tavriski Christian Institute (TCI), located in Kherson, to combine the work of running the school with thoughts of the possibility of war. In 2022, TCI was getting ready to celebrate its twenty-fifth anniversary. Our organization was entering a more stable phase of life—that's what we believed! Therefore, we were planning to hold a celebration conference in September. For the anniversary, we began to renovate our office area. We were planning to install a geothermal pump for our heating system. We bought sports equipment for summer camps. We added landscaping to beautify the TCI campus before the arrival of our guests. This cozy place on the bank of the Dnieper River, bought in 2003 at auction, always attracted the unwanted attention of corrupt businessmen and government workers. But the Lord showed us mercy in our legal fight with the unrighteous people who tried to take that place away from TCI, and we have succeeded in defending our right to ownership of that piece of land!

The preparation continued. We cleaned the bank of the river. During the Soviet Union times, the craggy cliffs bordering the Dnieper were covered with dirt. We wanted to restore their natural look. We washed off the dirt with water cannons till the rock base showed, then we made a hanging terrace and put tiles all along the embankment. Then we planned to set up gazebos and benches and add more lights and greenery. Each thought was linked to the desire to celebrate the quarter-century anniversary well. We had gone through many trials and successes, failures and achievements. One of the major events was receiving the state license in 2019. For the first time in the history of Ukraine, an evangelical educational institution received such a distinction! "Thus far the Lord has helped us"!

We anticipated to welcome partners, friends, and graduates of TCI at our celebration. The institute had educated many church ministers. We were also involved in translation and publishing and had a small printing office. The Pioneer Bible Translators (PBT) worked at our campus. We even had a small farm (hothouses) that supplied our kitchen with fresh vegetables. TCI also served in the countries of the Caucasus and Central Asia for years. We were hoping to publish a brochure with twenty-five stories of our graduates working for the kingdom of God. We expected many of them to come to the conference in the fall and share in our joy.

Everything was going well, but the "smell of war" was growing stronger.

My heart was often troubled. Since 2021 I had been strongly encouraged to evacuate with my family three times. But I felt responsible for my colleagues and students, so I continued to work. The Lord must have seen my concerns and unwillingness to leave Kherson, so he prompted Ethan Norton,* one of my friends from the United States, to prepare TCI staff for the possible upcoming crisis.

I have known Ethan Norton for a long time. About ten years ago, our institute held a retreat for pastors who had gone through persecution and imprisonment in one of the Central Asian countries. That event, which took place at the Black Sea, was made possible thanks to the support of ministers and counselors from the USA. Ethan stood out among the other members of the team. Tall, physically strong, wise, and sensible. Everything indicated that he was a military man, and that turned out to be true. He was involved in counterintelligence and antiterrorist activity. It was very pleasant to talk to him and see his deep faith. Also, he had a very unusual take on life. I was surprised to hear stories about his family. For example, Ethan never bought toy weapons for his children. At the same time, once a week he trained them in the use of real weapons, so that they could protect their family if needed. I recalled my childhood. We were raised in the spirit of the evangelical Baptists, so we were also not allowed to play with toy guns. But we were not taught the importance of using weapons for protection. I liked the approach of Ethan Norton. His

* Not his real name.

children would never play with weapons carelessly, but in the time of danger they would be able to protect themselves, their family, and their country.

Shortly before the Russian invasion, Ethan got in touch with me. He offered to help create a safety strategy for TCI in case of war. Using metaphors and biblical stories, Ethan communicated important truths. I remember looking at the experience of Paul from a new, unexpected perspective. The apostle was very different from other disciples of Christ. All the first apostles had one thing in common when it came to ministry: they waited for the Lord himself to guide them. But Paul made a plan and worked on implementing it. Thus, he remains in history as the most productive minister, and the key to his success is his strategy.

"War," explained Ethan, "always implies more risks, but a well-developed plan decreases the danger for all the staff."

I was happy that TCI had now such a spiritual mentor who was competent in that area. He became our safety consultant. Several other foreign organizations proposed detailed steps of evacuation. My colleagues and I had to make a plan and get each TCI worker familiar with it.

Of course, the words of the Lord came alive for me: "Suppose one of you wants to build a tower. Won't you first sit down and estimate the cost to see if you have enough money to complete it?" I began to understand that it was better to start taking care of safety beforehand than to be caught unprepared later, that it was wiser to be cautious earlier than to be sorry later. But, to tell the truth, it was difficult to try to be a man preparing for possible calamities. I did not mind working on evacuation strategy. But it was scary to think of what could happen next: What if the crisis did come and the plan would have to be implemented? I remember one of the points in the document sent to me: "Employers in profit and nonprofit organizations are responsible for the safety and health care of employees wherever the latter find themselves during work." Those words struck me as urgent and prompted me to hurry up.

The first meetings with colleagues were hard. Of course, the heads of the departments that formed our working team supported me. But the routine that followed was trying. I had to face criticism all the time. It has always been acceptable at TCI to express any criticism openly, so the colleagues felt free to argue, "Let's just keep working. Stop panicking!"

The situation pushed me into stupor and confusion. Besides, the line that separated me from excessive fearmongering looked very fine. I had to look for the right words to encourage my colleagues. The process would continue but then again encounter "soft resistance," so familiar to me. After all, it was just recently that I myself set up the same barriers while receiving the recommendations from Ethan Norton. Ethan showed patience. Now it was my turn to do the same. I encouraged my colleagues. The work continued. The minutes and hours spent in discussion ran fast. We would finish another step, and then someone would say, "How about just getting back to work?"

The frustration of my colleagues seemed natural, because their work had to be put on hold while we were preparing for possible crisis. I could understand them too well.

"Colleagues," I would tell them. "Today this is the most necessary work for us." Ignoring the preparation, we put at risk not only ourselves. Since TCI was closely connected with foreigners, we might have to face unnecessary risks that would result in reputational losses for our partners. "I am afraid to think," I said, my voice betraying my anxiety, "that the Russians could take one of you hostage and start to blackmail our foreign friends demanding money. We would put our partners in a difficult situation."

Praise be to God, more and more often I detected agreement in our team and the desire to keep our institute safe. Soon the document was ready. I wanted to breathe a sigh of relief and go back to my work. But it was very important to instruct each TCI worker and to create concrete signals that would alert us to the beginning of evacuation.

"The biggest danger once the plan is made"—the voice of Ethan Norton rang in my head—"is the postponement of evacuation. You should act resolutely even if a danger seems to have subsided and you feel 'easier.'"

I never thought that as a seminary worker I would be looking at a map not to see where TCI graduates were spreading God's Word but to mark the possible routes of invasion of the enemy. The location of Kherson made it vulnerable to attack on all sides. Therefore, we marked with red flags the three regions that could alert us to danger. If Russia invades from Crimea, then the village of Chaplynka will give a signal. If the Russians come from Donetsk region, the city of Melitopol will do that. And if the army comes from Transnistria and captures Chornomorsk or Odesa—this will be the sign that we need to evacuate.

How hard it was to look at the familiar names of villages and cities and feel forced to imagine a horrible scenario of war. I confess that it was very difficult to break the inertia of my thinking that tried to convince me that the invasion would not come, although the "lessons" of the Crimea and Donbas were still fresh in my memory.

During all the following meetings we were explaining the evacuation plan to the staff. Discussing potential dangers, we were preparing the people for the right reaction to the crisis. Ancient wisdom states, "If you falter in a time of trouble, how small is your strength." Thus, we strengthened the weak points in order to be able to handle the challenge well. It was some time before certain workers started to take the preparation seriously. At the beginning, it was common to hear familiar sentiments like "Stop panicking." However, the numerous meetings we held served as a good drill. We talked about personal responsibility during evacuation, about the necessity for each person to be ready. Every worker had to have an emergency suitcase and take care of his belongings, including phones, batteries, adapters, flashlights.

As an organization, TCI guaranteed to bring our staff and their families to a safe region. We had already reserved rooms at the regional union of the city of Ivano-Frankivsk located in the west of the country. People also knew that in case TCI failed to help them because of unexpected threats, they would have to get to Ivano-Frankivsk themselves and find our contact person. For those who wanted to have the evacuation plan on paper, we prepared printouts with a detailed description of necessary steps and contact information.

I had to constantly keep in my mind the number of people we were able to evacuate. Therefore, I suggested that four families move to the west of Ukraine beforehand. Two of them agreed. We bought them tickets for the date, which turned out to be the day of the invasion. The suddenness of the events prevented them from leaving, but that very fact was a confirmation of our willingness to hold to the evacuation plan. I am afraid even to think what would have happened had we not been prepared. I remember the letter I wrote to our friends and partners on January 28. It was sent several weeks before the war and helped people prepare without unnecessary panic. The English have a proverb, "The strength of the chain is in the weakest link." That's why we made every effort to strengthen each TCI worker.

Naturally, the drills helped us determine who could be given responsibilities for the evacuation. In order to be able to leave the city within twenty-four hours, we decided beforehand who would be responsible for what. One person was to get the people out, another to take care of finances, yet another to keep statutory documents, seals, and other valuables safe.

This is how our leadership in crisis was getting crystallized in the process.

Meanwhile, the "smell" of war was turning into a horrible concentrate of evil. It was becoming all-pervasive. No one could escape it. At such moments, everything turns dark and it's easy to fall into despair. So people reacted to what was happening in different ways: some got terrified, others remained unruffled, yet others acted as comforters—false comforters, as it turned out.

I remember a person coming to me with a prophecy that there would be no war so there was no need to panic. It was February 22. I was confused and did not know how to act. There was all the preparation for evacuation on one pan of the scales, and now there was a prophecy from a man who had been my friend for years on the other. But I did not hesitate for long. Sure, I wanted to take into consideration all the factors and pay attention to each new circumstance. I answered politely that the analysis and evaluation of the risks would not distract me from the most important thing, which was my work and carrying out the TCI mission.

It is one thing to have to deal with a prophecy, but it is quite another one to get a call from a bank worker who strongly recommends that you take all your money from the bank. It happened on Wednesday, February 23. I had to act resolutely. We were able to get everything from our safe deposit box just a few hours before the bank closed. Later that night, the banker himself called me. "Valentyn Serhiyovych," he said. "I want to make sure that you have taken all your valuables from your safe deposit box."

It was nice to hear that, yet it also made me sad. It seemed like some people in Kherson knew how things were really standing. There were rumors in the city that the police and several other institutions had already evacuated and taken all their documents with them. It looked like a betrayal by security agencies, and it was a hard blow on the locals. By the end of the day, even more disturbing news came. One of our pastors was returning from Henichesk to Kherson and noticed that the hydroelectric station in Kakhovka was not guarded. All the checkpoints on the way were also deserted. Many chaplains and volunteers confirmed that the army retreated in the evening. Such news definitely "smelled" of trouble and danger. Reality loomed larger.

My wife and I had nothing to do but to entrust the next day to the Lord and go to bed.

Chapter 2

Evacuation

"HOME" IS JUST FOUR LETTERS PLACED close to one another, but what a global meaning is contained in them. What an infinite essence it is! When we dare to think ourselves happy, we never exclude the possibility of this happening in the warm atmosphere of a home. We cannot remove home from this equation. Ancient Greeks used the word *oikos* when they spoke of family, property, and, of course, home per se. The prodigal son dreamed of leaving a foreign country and returning to his father's house—and his wish came true! Instead of a usual interjection, he joyfully breathed out "home" at the threshold! It is easy to explain man's love for his place of habitation—it's his home! There is no protection more desirable than the walls of one's home, so the English proverb "My home is my castle" stands true in all times.

But is there something more terrible than to wake up and find that war has encroached on the most sacred thing a man has—his life? Home will not save. How merciless are these currents of paralyzing terror at the first moments of awakening. Animal fear and stupor prevent your mind from grasping what is going on. You have been taken aback. I'm afraid to imagine how helpless my family would have felt on February 24 in our home, had we not been preparing for a possible disaster during the previous several months.

"Valik," my wife exclaimed with a start, using a diminutive form of my name. "What is it?"

"Sounds like explosions!"

An alarming rumbling grew clearer and louder. Faraway flashes were quickly approaching, glowing brightly in the morning mist. It was the monstrous face of war revealing itself to everyone.

I picked up my phone. It was not even 5 a.m. Luba was not in a hurry to wake up the children—she did not want to frighten them.

Our dog Sherri was whimpering anxiously. I dialed the number of Leonid Matseyka, the first vice president of TCI, who had been in charge of all the administrative matters for the last five years.

"It has begun," I said. "Let's follow the plan!"

"It has begun!" was the response.

Sometimes one phrase is enough to describe the whole state of affairs. Details will become clear later. The most important thing to be communicated is that it has begun! We need to act according to the plan. Leonid is responsible for reaching the members of the administrative department. I begin to notify my brothers, one of whom lives next door. I call my parents.

"It has begun!"

The cover of darkness is torn, the lights are turned on in the houses. The exclamations, "It has begun," can be heard all throughout the sleepy city, and the meaning of tragic events is revealed to everyone with the preciseness of a military report.

"Stas," I call to my brother, who is also a youth minister in our church. "It has begun," I breathe out.

Now the steps of our evacuation plan for which he is responsible come to life for him as well. I am sure that he will take care of the logistics and transportation. I hear my wife telling her sister urgently on the phone, "Maryna, you have to leave now." Kakhovka is an hour away from our city. Maryna had to leave her house immediately and join us so that we could evacuate together—this has been the plan.

"Maryna, hurry!" Luba urges.

I see that she is worried about her sister. I want to know more about what is going on. I find the phone number of one of the pastors who live near the border with Crimea. Oleksandr Kobzar is a graduate of our institute. He has been serving in Chaplynka for the last several years.

"Valentyn, I have already evacuated; left just as I was. I have not taken anything with me—like 'a burning stick snatched from the fire.' I got a call at 4 a.m. and they told me, 'You have less than half an hour—the Russians have already crossed the border.'"

It was also important for me to call my former fellow-student Yevhen Bondarenko. We have been friends for a quarter of a century. I knew he always stayed in touch with the military.

"They are already in Chaplynka, Valentyn," he said with a sad voice, confirming the invasion of the Russians into Ukraine.

"Hold on, friend!"

I ended the call. The day was dawning timidly. It is scary to imagine in such moments that at those very hours the innocence of the morning is torn not by the rays of the rising sun but by the flashes of explosions. The calls made as well as the coordination of the evacuation indicated that it was going to be a hard day. The children were already up. I saw a touch of fear in their eyes. But still, both son and daughter did not lose their nerve. They were helping their mother, making occasional calls in the process. I hugged my wife tenderly.

"Luba, make a breakfast, please." I remembered the sadness in the voice of my friend from Kakhovka. "I don't know when I will be able to eat at our house again."

Soon the aroma of fried eggs, sausage, and coffee fill our cozy kitchen. Everything is done quickly and cursorily. Cooking is interrupted by calls to and from colleagues and remaining packing. No pauses. Concentration. Time flies. No tarrying. It is already 6:30 a.m. The family hastily gathers around the breakfast table. We eat earlier than usual today. I notice forks and knives laid out by my wife on the tablecloth. In the time of hurried preparations and approaching war, everything touches and pains your heart in a special way. Savoring that sweet comfort, we need to strengthen ourselves with food before facing enormous challenges.

We were all to meet at the Church of Christ the Savior at 11 a.m. Stas, Leonid, and I were responsible for most of the things. Oleksandr, my younger brother, joined us later. Leonid was taking care of TCI documents. It was necessary to destroy personal files of our students; after all, some of them were not from Ukraine. It could endanger them in the countries where they served. We decided to take the diplomas of the graduates with us. It was dangerous to delay our departure. The enemy was drawing closer. At around 8 a.m., an alarming call came from Kakhovka. It was my wife's sister.

"Luba, it's hopeless." Maryna sounded upset. "Tanks are already at the Northern Crimean canal, and armored cars are going along my street, they have V and Z letters on them. Luba, do you know what these marks mean?"

No one knew what they meant then. And no matter how they were interpreted later, they will remain in the memory of each Ukrainian as symbols of the terror of Russia's treacherous invasion.

Maryna was not able to get out of Kakhovka. She decided to stay and support her close friend and her friend's elderly mother. It was an unexpected turn of events. One can only imagine what the sisters felt. War does not take you into consideration; it just intrudes and changes your plans. It cuts to the quick. It knows it has the upper hand. So it is a great challenge to act against it, following the evacuation plan without any delays!

I was just recovering from that alarming news when another phone call announced a new turn of events.

"Valentyn." It was my brother Stas. His voice betrayed anxiety. "The drivers refuse to take us out of Kherson!"

"What?!"

An important item of the evacuation protocol flashed before my eyes: we have an agreement with the drivers of minivans as well as their names and phone numbers.

"They are afraid for their families—anything could happen to their close ones remaining in the city while they are away."

"Stas, tell them they can bring their families along!"

"OK!"

The long minutes of negotiations seem endless. People have suddenly changed their minds. It is understandable. It is one thing to promise something in the time of peace, and quite another to face the reality of war that invades the city and threatens each inhabitant. Everyone is scared. No one knows what to do, which step to make.

We failed to persuade the drivers. I could almost feel the air around me thickening. It would take an effort to get through its denseness. If some little news can make you fall into stupor, what about constantly changing events? It is easy to feel vulnerable at such moments. To give up. But we need to act!

"Well, then, we need to buy a van to evacuate people!"

The car market was crowded. By 9 a.m. people were hastily purchasing minivans, parting with their last savings in order to leave the city. We could hear faraway explosions from time to time. But the seller looked calm despite all the alarming signals. He seemed unbothered by everything that was going on around him. "Whether the war begins or not," he said while treating us to coffee, "we have to do business." We were surprised. He was so different from the thousands of civilians, including ourselves, who were in a hurry to evacuate.

We saw a white Mercedes Sprinter that could accommodate fifteen to nineteen people. It would suit us perfectly! We did not have to wonder long why nobody had bought it yet: it had flat tires and wouldn't start at the first try. We agreed on the price. Then there was a problem of the registration: both police and organizations that dealt with the registration had already left the city. The seller gave us registration papers and a confirmation that the van was not stolen but bought for TCI needs. I never thought a thing like that was possible, and we praised the Lord!

We had an hour left before the appointed time. Despite all our efforts, we were behind schedule. New circumstances kept arising. After we had filled the tires, it turned out that there was no gas in the tank. There was already a shortage of gas and diesel fuel in the city, and we had to fill the tank for the journey. Only those who have been through similar experience can understand the despair one feels at such moments.

The solution came unexpectedly—it was a miracle!

My brother Oleksandr decided to call the firm he worked for. The company owned a lot of trucks and delivered building materials all around the region. Oleksandr drove one of those trucks.

"Yes, yes, we are taking women and children out of the city," he was telling the owner on the phone, and a second later he was crying out joyfully, "Thank you! God bless you!"

We got permission to use the gas left in the truck that Oleksandr drove. The generosity of the man sent by heaven made it possible to gas up the van and take sixty liters of diesel fuel with us. We said a prayer for that man. The danger was approaching, and he, as the owner of the firm, had to think of what to do with his car park, which the enemy could confiscate.

Almost each year in the last decade we enjoyed a mild February. On the day of our evacuation the weather was wonderful. It affected our packing decisions. My wife did not even bring a scarf. It was also difficult to decide which things we would need and which not. Although we had all the bare necessities in our emergency suitcase, what do we do with pets? To many of us, the four-legged are family members. So, it was decided to leave behind the family photo album that contained the pictures from the time of our wedding. That family treasure always held a special place in our hearts. But that album with a blue cover as well as our favorite books had to stay home. I did not even bring the clothes I wore to church. But we did bring our cat and dog. Like many other people, we had no idea what difficulties we were going to encounter soon—not only during the journey but also in Ivano-Frankivsk, where it turned out to be hard to find an apartment whose owners would accept renters with pets.

The trunk of our car was not very spacious, so we could not take much. The contents of my travel bag showed how limited our luggage was: a couple of shirts, something casual, two pairs of jeans, a sweater, socks, underwear, a laptop, and documents. I did not even have time to pack myself—Luba did it for me while I was buying the van for evacuation.

CHAPTER 2

I walked around the house, shut off water and gas. I looked into each room to make sure all the windows were closed and the electrical appliances turned off. Suddenly my eye caught sight of black marks on the doorpost in the kitchen. My heart skipped a beat. The scenes of the past flashed before my eyes. Every year my son and daughter stood at the doorpost and I would mark their height with a pencil as a sign of a new stage in their lives. I touched those dear dashes and prayed, entrusting our house and future into God's hands. That was how I would pray every time I was going on a business trip. That day everyone had to leave home at the same time, which was unusual for us. We preferred the settled way of life. Now we were setting on a long journey, and the Maker alone knew what it would be like.

Our Ford gave way under the weight of the luggage. My son and daughter were in the backseat together with Yaroslav, my future son-in-law. The suddenness of Russian invasion dealt a hard blow to the plans of the kids—they were both engaged. And now they were facing a hurried evacuation with the war breathing down their necks. My son failed to persuade the parents of his fiancée to let her go with us. The daughter was luckier—her fiancé came along. We were crowded in the car with our dog Sherri—a cross between a Pekinese and a Bolognese—scurrying between us, and a carrier with a cat held in the lap.

We came with our brothers and our wives to our parents' house to say good-bye. I got out of the car. I remembered several farewell meetings in this yard. When two of my brothers and my sister moved abroad, all our families gathered there to say good-bye. There are seven of us children, all grown up. And now we were forced to part. Before, saying good-bye was not marred by the anxiety of war, but that day it was accompanied by explosions. It was unimaginably hard. Mom was crying softly. Dad and I did not say much to each other. He was in poor health: cancer, constant insomnia. For months I had been trying to talk him into going with us.

"Take the students out, Son," he would always say. "I am staying with the church. Someone has to minister here, especially to those who have not yet found the faith in the Lord."

We prayed. When I was getting back into the car, the explosions that had been far away were closer, and louder. I broke into a cold sweat. Sherri was restless: even in the times of peace she disliked fireworks and firecrackers at the festivals. Every time she heard them, she would hide and whimper. Now, just like us, the dog was hearing something terrible.

Anxious anticipation accompanied with sorrow permeated the atmosphere of the meeting point at the Church of Christ the Savior. This can usually be felt when you look into the future, not knowing what it holds. After all, it is one thing to "model" a future crisis, imagine possible circumstances, try on the most reasonable response, and then go and enjoy the fruits of a peaceful life. But it is quite another thing to be besieged by troubles.

I could read the facial expressions of the people and understand what each of them was thinking. It was painful to see. We were all facing evacuation. Everyone was to contribute to its quality, speed, and efficiency. That's why we had been working for months to train our team. Now our big group had to leave for western Ukraine in an orderly fashion. It would be impossible without mutual trust. The disaster did not spare those who were unprepared. Yet it united at the same time. I saw the kindness with which people rushed to help one another.

I remember a woman in an arctic fox coat. She was so distressed by what was going on that she could not control herself. Her husband was a seaman, away from home at the time. She was alone with her old mother. When she heard the front approaching, she put her mother in the car and wanted to leave but found her gas tank empty. She managed to get a five-liter can of gasoline, but she was too nervous to fill the tank by herself. I helped her and she left.

Everyone was busy with something: bags were being repacked and stacked compactly; the people who were arriving met up, roll calls were made. It was important to keep the list of people in my head, to assign the seats in the van and also to send a message to

Ivano-Frankivsk, where we had rooms reserved for us. Some teammates with cars had already left the city by themselves. Long before the evacuation, TCI paid salaries to the workers in advance. Since the salaries are not high at our institute, we decided to allocate additional money to the employees if they needed it during the move. On the day of the evacuation, only one family asked for it.

But it was the people who broke emotionally at the sound of explosions who gave us the most trouble. Despite all the preparations, they did not find strength to overcome the stupor, leave their homes, and converge from around the city at our meeting point. We kept calling them, trying to persuade them, looking for the right words. Of course, we had included steps in our plan for those who decided to stay. So the people knew what to buy, how to act, what to do. But the responsibility for each member of the team troubled us—we did everything we could! Later, the evacuated people recalled with gratitude that it was our insistence that helped them break free from fear and make a decision. "You have saved us!" they told us later. But at the moment, each minute lost affected our departure, putting us behind schedule.

The stress was overwhelming. I remember a man and his pregnant wife who were going to leave with us. They came with a small bag and a backpack and got into the van. After three or four blocks, they suddenly asked to be let out.

"Sorry, we are not ready to leave," they said. "We are not ready for evacuation; it is hard for us, we are very sorry!"

How unimaginably hard it is to leave people in unsafe places! Later I found out that they were helped by the embassy of Israel, because the husband was a Jew. The family moved to Israel and had a baby there. We were happy for them. But there were cases when leaving people meant never seeing them again!

We left the Church of Christ the Savior at 1 p.m. It was frightening. The scene around us sunk deep into our hearts, and it seemed there was no hope it would ever surface. But every time we remembered the day we left the city, the details of evacuation would come back to us. The sky was torn by explosions. The war washed the people out of the cities as a relentless stream; the hustle in the streets was very different from the daily routine of a peaceful life. Cars were rushing, carried by a raging whirlwind. A great noise was made by the vehicles, and the yells of people filled the air. At the outskirts of the city, all that chaos transformed into a slow-moving funnel. The vehicles departing the city were divided into two and, at times, three lanes.

The country landscape was saying good-bye to us. The weather was nice, but it was powerless to warm up the hearts frozen because of the cold—the cold of war. The signs of war were everywhere. We could see two helicopters above us all the time. It was impossible to determine whether those "birds" belonged to our army or to the enemy. But the logic was simple: since they did not bomb us, they may have been Ukrainian. The same feelings were provoked by the armored cars we met on the way. The iron "stallions" without markings. It made you wonder whether they were Russian or Ukrainian. We used the same logic: they did not shoot at us, so they belonged to our army. As civilians, we expect military machines to protect us, not to attack us—peaceful and unarmed people.

What is the smoke in the distance? Is it the airport?!

The sight of the burning airport in Chornobaivka village hit us hard. How could that be? For many years, that "air gate" of Kherson meant a lot to me personally. I always planned my international trips so I would fly out of and into Chornobaivka. And now the airport was destroyed by Russian rockets. Black soot hovered over the steppe. The hope that "everything will be as it was" was vanishing like those clouds of smoke. Sad reality affirmed that all we had been used to was changed—for a long time, and maybe forever.

Panic seemed to be driving people so hard that nobody paid attention to a group of soldiers on the side of the road trying to hitch a lift. As soon as they noticed our van, they began to wave their hands. After seeing armored cars and helicopters on the way, one does not feel like responding to the calls of soldiers in full ammunition.

Stas was driving the van. Something in the behavior of the soldiers seemed strange to him. He pulled to the side of the road and cautiously rolled down the window. Ten or fifteen soldiers wearing Ukrainian army chevrons ran up to him.

"Help us, Pops!"

That address just killed us—"Pops." We were looking at a group of draftees. Eighteen-year-old boys. Now, months later, it is still a mystery to me what those kids were doing in Chornobaivka without their commanding officers. They could not have been deserters. The draftees do not usually take part in battles.

"We have an order to move to Mykolaiv."

While a boy was explaining which military base they had to go to, I was looking into the faces of the young soldiers. I could see my son Kirill in each of them. He was just a little older, a university student. My father's heart was moved by the sight of the boys. Why are they hitchhiking here, abandoned by their officers? They are barely out of high school. One of them may have planned to become an IT person after military service, while another dreamed of becoming a lawyer. Still another may have intended to return home and help his father at the farm. Sure, some of them may have wanted to remain in the army, but real battles are hardly the best way to start a military career. How can one avoid feeling revolted at the war initiated by the neighbor. It is the war that destroyed the habitual way of life and daily routine. It was hard to look into the eyes of the boys, see their fear, and hear confusion in their voices. "Help us, Pops!"

"Get into the bus, boys!" ordered Stas.

It was hard to observe what was happening and realize that war was metastasizing across our country. How unbearable it is to come to terms with the feeling of helplessness—the inability to aid our motherland in the hour of trouble. The thought that we were taking a group of civilians out in an orderly fashion created a false sense of guilt. We did not think of the utmost significance of our important mission at the time. We just wanted to get to a safe place. All we needed to do was to step on the gas. That was what thousands and thousands of drivers leaving Kherson were doing. It was several hours before we reached Mykolaiv, although before, such a journey would take half as long. The overcrowded road did not allow us to go fast. Besides, there were car accidents on the way. We had to wait. Take detours. The soldiers stood without complaint in the van during the whole journey. When we were nearing Mykolaiv, some people wanted to buy food for them. But the draftees refused. Bound by the order of their officer, they were in a hurry to get to the military base.

Armored cars, helicopters, a ruined airport, draftees—each war sign encountered on the way was distressing, but some unexpected inner strength helped to overcome the torture of the first hours of the evacuation. There was a deep-set hope that all the tragedy raging in our land would not last long. We will come home. Everything will be as before . . .

It was already long after noon. We were getting really hungry. After all, we breakfasted early, and a small cup of coffee at the car market did not count. We wanted to eat. Since we were behind schedule, it was important to hurry. I thought that somewhere an Englishman was on his way to work after breakfast. In the other part of the world, an American was still in his bed at the crack of dawn while we Ukrainians were rushing forward, looking into the vastness of the Kherson steppes as if into the future. There was only the unknown before us. As we caught sight of leafless trees, road signs, and village houses, our hearts swelled with emotion and we swallowed back our tears, counting the miles of evacuation.

Phone calls pulled us out of our reveries. We stayed in touch with our fellow evacuees in other cars. My partners and friends also called. Everyone was interested in what was happening. Some asked to comment on the war. Some calls proved to be life-changing later: one of the phone conversations with Taras Dyatlik impacted TCI work during the war.

As soon as the calls stopped, I felt oppressed. It was hard to cope with the situation. My wife was crying softly. I wanted to hear music.

Something to distract us. We could not listen to the radio. I looked for some music and found Cory Asbury's song called "Egypt." It was about the exodus of God's people. The youth in our church loved that composition and sang it in Ukrainian. As it turned out later, "Egypt" was played in many cars of the refugees that day.

The hymn brought comfort. We played it over and over again, listening to the story of how Yahweh took his people by the hand and delivered them to the promised land. I suddenly realized that the Bible text referred to the events similar to what we Ukrainians were facing now. There was an odd and indescribable sense of affinity with those whom God helped in strange lands. I remembered Ruth, Esther, Daniel and his friends. Suddenly, I thought that Jesus's parents were also forced to leave Judea when danger arose. Then I remembered my visit to Xavier University in Cincinnati, Ohio, where I saw an icon depicting the holy family. I was surprised to see Joseph, Mary, and Jesus dressed as contemporary refugees. At that time, the world was facing a migration crisis caused by the war in Syria, and the artist painted that scene from the gospel, clearly indicating that the Lord had known by experience what it was like to be a refugee.

Then, right there, at the wheel, I had a revelation: the Lord Jesus had been a displaced person in Bethlehem, a refugee, just like each of us was now! Even though I had read the Bible since childhood, I never experienced such emotions. I was stunned by that revelation. I could feel it with all my being that Christ was a displaced person! I was a displaced person! We were all displaced people!

Chapter 3

Westbound

SOMETIMES YOU WISH YOU WERE A BIRD that sees everything that is happening on Earth from on high. You can almost feel the rapture of shooting upward! The closer to white clouds you get, the better you can observe life below. All that is visible on Earth is like a carpet underneath you. There is a vast steppe cut by shallow ravines. The Dnieper River spreads out its arms. Mosaics of houses and gardens. The ribbons of roads look like serpents along which cars are rushing to somewhere.

With three lines of cars moving slowly out of the city, with some vehicles even getting into the incoming lane, it would be good to rise above it all and look around. To see what is impeding the traffic: checkpoints, abandoned vehicles that everyone has to drive around, car accidents—anything can happen when people are in a hurry. Or are the cars so close to one another that it limits the speed? It would also be helpful to look at the places from which all these people are forced to flee today.

Kherson! How are you, dear city? How close is the front to you now? Will all these hundreds of thousands of cars manage to get to safe places in time?

Our vehicles tried to keep together. We were driving in such a way that nobody could break our line and squeeze in between. We had two vans and four cars, two of which were electric. Their batteries lasted only for one hundred kilometers, then the cars had to be towed so they could be recharged. When I was leaving Kherson, my Ford did not have much gas. Outside the city, I saw an obscure old gas station where I could fill my tank. By that time, gas stations would sell only ten to twenty liters of gas per car. That was another miracle and an answer to our prayer! We set out on a journey without gas!

Of course, our travel was involuntary. Many Ukrainians living in the south of the country preferred a settled lifestyle. I often had to go abroad because of my work, taking five to six trips a year. But my family rarely left the city. Only during the last eight or nine years did we start to take one trip annually together. Now, our overloaded car was crawling along the road toward a part of Ukraine where we had never been before. It was not very comfortable, especially for the passengers in the backseat who had to deal with a dog and a cat. Sherri could stay calm, but the cat had to be given sedatives because he was restless in his cage. Sometimes we would let him out to stretch his legs. He would jump all around the car and then fall asleep on the dashboard. His cozy frame reminded us of the home left far behind.

Thus did our convoy continue to move west. We hoped to reach Uman by nightfall, but it became clear by the evening that it was not going to happen. It was already getting dark. Although we kept in touch with each other, a person sitting near the driver in each car was responsible for communication. Yet, somehow, I got separated from the rest of the convoy. GPS led me to the road to Kropyvnytskyi, while the rest of the vehicles kept following the Mykolaiv road. When we realized the error, it was too late to turn back. We agreed to spend the night at different locations.

I made some calls, and my friends referred me to a family with many children living in the suburbs of Kropyvnytskyi. Soon the anxiety one feels groping his way to the unknown was replaced with a sense of temporary happiness as we received a very warm welcome from our hosts that night. We were discovering new facets of people's hospitality, so coveted in the time of relocation. We were given two rooms on the second floor that were perfect for our family and pets.

We found out that our hosts were raising not only their four biological children but also two kids whose mother had died from COVID. Families with many children never cease to amaze me. They are very accepting. I myself was born and raised in a home with seven children. The night promised an unforgettable rest after our long journey. Simple food was set on the table: noodle soup, spaghetti, sausage. It looked like a royal feast! The hostess unassumingly put fancy tableware before us. My day began with an early breakfast, and I still remembered knives and forks lovingly laid out by my wife. Now hundreds of miles away from home, our evening meal was thoughtfully supplemented with a similar sign of hominess. It was impossible to miss it. That ended the first day of our wanderings.

We left early the next morning. It was February 25. Our hosts continued to show their care at the parting, trying to give us cookies and tea for the road. I admit, we were deeply touched by their hospitality and did not dare to take all the treats offered to us, accepting just a part of them. We were in some kind of stupor, unable to evaluate rationally how much strength we would need for the journey that day.

We were already on our way when we heard that the Russians had shelled Kropyvnytskyi that morning. Our hosts from the night before also had to evacuate. The war was catching up with us. It trampled new territories mercilessly with its dirty boots. It was dangerous to tarry.

We met with the other members of our team at about noon in Uman. They had spent the night in Yuzhnoukrainsk, in the house of a kind and righteous lady. I had met her at the conferences held in the south of Ukraine. She is a businesswoman with a small ranch with horses. She raises the animals to provide therapy for children who have problems with their musculoskeletal systems. This therapy that encourages sick children to spend time with animals is very effective. They begin to stretch as they try to pat a horse; they learn to care for the animal, and riding gives them a kind of massage that helps improve coordination and muscle strength. It was nice to hear about the hospitality of the lady. I thought there was a certain symbolism in that: she welcomed refugees who were suffering from paralysis caused by war, thus providing them with some healing.

And now we were bound to Chernivtsi. It was difficult to determine how much time it would take, because traveling during war is unpredictable. A six-and-a-half-hour trip can turn into a twelve-hour, exhausting adventure. Besides, we had to gas up our cars. By that time there was a problem with fuel in Ukraine. We heard that rich people were paying $100 for a can of gas to avoid spending hours in lines at gas stations. We tried to use our resources sparingly. The fact that we could leave Kherson with full tanks was encouraging. But we needed to replenish our resources. We also needed to nourish ourselves.

We made a stop in Uman to get some food. Hot dogs are a popular snack at gas stations. I remembered that our hosts in Kropyvnytskyi had offered us some refreshments for the road. Only now, suffering from hunger, were we able to appreciate their kindness fully. That's how we discovered a new aspect of war. It is capable of depriving a person of basic necessities—food, for example. Instead, it tortures you with hunger, exhausts you, takes away your strength, or even the most valuable thing of all, your life.

We were lucky to find a place for the night in the suburbs of Chernivtsi. A congregation in Vitryanka village was waiting to welcome us, but we were still on the road. The van bought in Kherson broke down several times on the way. We had to stand in the cold for long periods of time. The weather was becoming frosty, which southerners like us were not used to. The Mercedes could be jump-started, but by midnight, when we were very close to Chernivtsi, it broke down completely. We couldn't do anything with it. The city looked like a bustling place, which surprised us. Night roads were filled with vehicles, which showed that evacuation to the west continued. The last stage of our journey proved to be an adventure. Things looked hopeless, even though the van made it to a repair shop. It was night. All the mechanics were most likely in bed dreaming, although hardly a person in the country would have been able to sleep peacefully that night. We were overcome by the feeling of helplessness.

Then, out of the blue, there was a tall and strong man standing before us. He was curious to see who could be at the gates of his shop so late at night. He turned out to be the owner.

"What happened?" he asked.

"Our bus has broken, and we are evacuating children and women . . . ," Stas began.

He was not given a chance to finish.

"What are you, a priest?" the man interrupted. He was apparently impressed with my younger brother's long beard, which made Stas look like an Orthodox priest.

"Yes, I am a priest," Stas replied.

The man looked the passengers over, said a quick "wait," and made a call. A little later, the lights were on in the shop, and a mechanic arrived. It was another miracle. The owner managed to talk one of his workers into leaving his bed at 1 a.m. and coming to help us. The repairs took a couple of hours. As it turned out, the drive belt was torn. While it was being fixed, we made several runs, getting children and teenagers to Vitryanka, where the people had been waiting for us.

They did not lose time preparing for our coming. Within two days the congregation turned their prayer house into a shelter. Cots were put in the worship hall, which was heated so well that it was possible to sleep on the floor. We were allowed to take a dog and a cat into the church building. The hospitality of our hosts exceeded all expectations. The family with little children was invited to stay in somebody's house. Stas Vats was the youngest traveler among us. The child braved all the challenges of the move riding in the electric car with his parents.

How wonderful it was to fall asleep in safety and long-awaited warmth on the second night of our travels, reveling in the care of our brothers and sisters! And how touching it was to see the renewal of their care in the morning. At dawn, when we were just waking up, the prayer house was already bustling. Women came and brought a home-cooked meal. We will never forget the abundance of buckwheat with bacon and vegetables, pancakes, and fruit juice they fed us. In addition, they gave us two boxes of fruit for the road. Their area is famous for growing apples and pears. The locals usually gather the produce till the end of autumn in order to send it to the markets in Kyiv. Their fruit gifts were very welcome. Our supplies were running low, and the journey was not over yet. We did not know how tough the cold would be that day, but we were leaving with a solid resource of warmth produced by the love of hospitable inhabitants of Vitryanka.

The last stage of evacuation took place on Saturday, February 26. As we set out on our journey, we felt like an athlete who has to muster all his strength right before the finish line. Usually, it would take just a couple of hours to get to Ivano-Frankivsk from where we were, provided there was no heavy traffic. But when you are going as a part of a convoy, you need to take into consideration the needs of each member of the team. That day, the van bought in Kherson proved to be the weak link. Despite the repairs done the day before, it kept falling apart. The forced stops on the way were exhausting. We were on the road for three days already. Our final destination seemed to be just around the corner. So we decided to leave behind the problem van and use GPS to get to Ivano-Frankivsk in several cars by village roads, stopping at checkpoints on the way. We entered the city at twilight—the sun seemed to set earlier in that region—whether because of thick clouds or mountains. Evacuation was completed, and the new and unfamiliar world of Ivano-Frankivsk was opening before us refugees.

It is not easy to weigh anchor in a familiar haven and set sail to foreign lands even in times of peace. But the war caused many people to undertake the move. It took a lot of effort, time, and resources to get to a safe place. Our evacuation strategy, worked out in pains during long meetings, began to bear fruit once we got to Ivano-Frankivsk. Everything may not have gone as planned. We were not able to evacuate all the staff. The journey took longer than we had anticipated. The level of stress turned out to be high. It is scary even to think what would have happened had we not been preparing. The agreement TCI had made with Baptist churches in Ivano-Frankivsk regarding the lodgings helped us avoid additional stress and work. After all, the refugees from Luhansk, Chernihiv, Kharkiv, Sumy, and Kyiv were also coming to Ivano-Frankivsk at the time. The number of locations from which people were fleeing indicated the scale of the invasion.

The church in Ivano-Frankivsk had the apartments ready for us. The ministers bought washing machines, helped convert Sunday school classrooms into bedrooms, put beds and tables in the cafeteria. And, of course, an abundant dinner awaited us: borsch, bacon, dumplings—a warm welcome for the refugees exhausted after a long trip!

It did not go without incidents. A man, whom we later learned was a deacon in the church, hit our dog Sherri when my wife, Luba, was coming out of the cafeteria.

"Don't you know that animals are not allowed in the house of God?!"

It was really distressing for us newcomers. When you spend several days on the road, going through checkpoints, listening to the news of shelling in Ukraine on the radio, and finally get out of danger—hungry, unwashed, tired, but happy to be safe—you do not think the problem would be your pet, as someone forbids it to go not into a place where they hold worship services but into a cafeteria. That man was explaining to my wife the importance of revering the house of God for another good fifteen minutes.

I did not witness the incident because I was talking to the pastor about organizational matters in his office at the time. When my wife told me later, I was shocked. I could not believe that a man would just hit a dog so that "the rules would not be broken." That showed me that we and the inhabitants of the region had different cultures and traditions. Soon those differences became even more obvious, which prompted all of us—both refugees and locals—to try to become more flexible for the sake of peace.

The accommodation of the refugees lasted well into the night. The locals gave us their apartments for the families and refugees with children. Young people and students were housed on the third floor of a separately standing church building with a kitchen on the second floor. My family was the last one to get accommodation. Pastor Yaroslav generously offered us a three-room apartment where his mother had previously lived. We had other housing options but accepted Yaroslav's, and it proved to be a good choice. Soon, the refugees had to face difficulties related to the local peculiarities, and it turned out to be hard to find housing for people with pets. But my family was spared from all that. Besides, when my wife first walked into the apartment, she testified that it was exactly the lodgings she had been praying for. However, on the night of our move, we had a problem with our neighbor. As I was unloading the car, one of the drunken men began to act a bit strange.

"Where are you coming from?" he was yelling. "Why are you moving in without a permission from the military registration office?"

My explanations did not satisfy him. He immediately made a call and then passed the phone to me. "Here, talk!"

"I am a church minister, president of a Christian institute," I began to explain politely. "We brought a group of people from the Kherson region several hours ago."

"Everything is fine, make yourself comfortable," a reply came. "We do not draft priests."

I handed the phone back to its owner. I did not have to give further explanations—the man had heard the conversation. We shook hands and I continued to unload the car. The distress of my neighbor was easy to understand. It was the third day of the war. When you see a stranger around, you can't help asking yourself, "Why is this man not in the army? Is he trying to avoid being drafted? Is he a subversive?" Recently formed Territorial Defense patrols that checked the documents as well as the watchfulness of the locals like my angry neighbor were a part of a new reality. Nobody knew how long the war would last. But for now, I, my family, and TCI staff had to drop anchor here, in Ivano-Frankivsk, and stay open to life-changing events. And those were not long in coming!

Chapter 4

Acceptance

THE YELLOW WALLS OF A CATHEDRAL with a low steeple were almost completely hidden by the morning mist that filled the streets of the city. Locals and tourists have been admiring this sanctuary for centuries. Some just appreciate it as a historical site, while the church cherishes it as its second home.

It was Sunday, February 27. Our group of refugees, though very tired, was hurrying to the worship service. As soon as we crossed the threshold, we saw the date of the construction of the building inscribed in the mosaic floor. Before, the cathedral belonged to the Roman Catholic Church, but for the last thirty years it has been a property of a Baptist congregation.

Once in the building, we realized how cold, dark, and depressing it was outside. Inside we were enveloped by warmth. Yellow and green walls were decorated with reliefs. There were rows of wooden chairs on both sides of the central aisle. Near the altar there were benches instead of chairs. There was also a balcony in the worship hall with two wooden staircases leading to it. A beautiful chandelier was hanging from the ceiling. In front, there was a banner with a text from the Bible between arched windows, and underneath, three rows of chairs for the choir set at different levels, a piano, and a pulpit.

Our group was given a place in the worship hall itself. Despite warm greetings, we could see poorly hidden concern in people's faces. It was not only because of the news about the war. Among the church members and guests were refugees from different parts of Ukraine who witnessed the tragedy unfolding. Within just a few days, the war cut down their roots and broke their ties with the homeland. The war hurled them into strange territories, thousands of miles away from home—try and live with it!—and made sure they would constantly feel painfully lonely, even here, inside the walls of the cathedral.

The worship service began. The choir traditionally started with hymns. It was incredibly hard to sing today. It seemed difficult to process your thoughts and feelings while fully participating in the worship, knowing that the war had been raging in the country for four days already. Serhiy Dovhoniuk, the senior pastor, had a hard task of encouraging the people present with his sermon. In its essence, the sermon is meant to give people answers, so each heart would be able to receive a wise edification and to rest in God's peace. But typical messages do not always fit well with the times of trouble. Tragedy seemed to be more powerful than the pastoral consolation. Everything may have looked the same to the locals, but the refugees could not shake off anxiety. When you face a calamity alone, it is hard to absorb fully the words coming from the pulpit. Some cried through the entire worship service.

"Brothers and sisters," said the pastor in the end. "I would like you to meet Valentyn Syniy."

Deep in my thoughts, I did not expect to be called to the stage.

"He is a pastor of the church and president of a Christian institute. Yesterday he and many others came from Kherson to our city!"

I was invited to come forward. I was used to addressing all kinds of audiences, from small gatherings to large conference crowds. But the words of thanks I conveyed to the inhabitants of Ivano-Frankivsk were spoken with great emotion, as I observed hundreds of eyes filled with tears.

"I thank each of you with all my heart for welcoming the people of Kherson!"

Then the pastor asked our people to stand so that others could pray for them. It was then that differences became obvious: none of our women was wearing a headscarf, while it was a "must" for the ladies of that church to cover their heads. Two of our brothers stood out because of their full beards, and one of them had a shaved head besides.

Despite those differences, Serhiy's prayer was warm and kind, and it made us feel at home, which was necessary and valuable at the moment. A refugee is vulnerable in many ways: he has no home, no relatives, no friends, no connections. There is no work and, therefore, no provision. He is under stress because of what is going on, and he needs strength to handle the upcoming challenges. Of course, the whole world is open to him, offering new opportunities in life, but a newcomer is always a stranger if no one makes him feel accepted by doing little things for him. It is hard to stand alone. And although we stayed as a group, we needed the prayers of the local church.

I am sure that the prayer of the senior pastor encouraged the church to show leniency to the refugees and accept us despite the differences. Many people responded and came up to us after the service. Some encouraged us with words, others shared food. We could feel their care, support, and attention.

But the war kept marching through the land. Every day more and more refugees came to the west of Ukraine. In the beginning, churches alone helped the newcomers. It was only later that various organizations and governmental services joined the efforts to solve the problems. Kindergarten, school, and hospital buildings in various places began to be used to house the refugees. But initially all the responsibility was laid on Christian communities. We were among the first ones to enjoy the hospitality and care of the churches in Ivano-Frankivsk, yet we had no desire whatsoever to become a burden to the people who had welcomed us. TCI helped the church to pay utilities for the building where we had rooms for staff, a cafeteria, and several offices. Neither did we exclude ourselves from helping other refugees, even though we were refugees too. So, already on the next day, February 28, we started assisting the church in feeding people. We paid two cooks from the church and we bought groceries. The members of the congregation also brought home-canned vegetables. What started with five tables for our staff from Kherson grew into feeding over a hundred people daily. Not only refugees but also the homeless came to our cafeteria.

I remember what a blessing that active ministry became for us. It rescued us as it kept our mind from thinking about what was happening in the country. But at times stress became unbearable. It was impossible to feel peace in your heart when you saw thousands and thousands of frightened people fleeing from all over the country to the west, which was the safest place in Ukraine for the time being. It was impossible to predict what would happen next. The news from the front was discouraging. The war was wearing people out, so they ran to Poland and other European countries that opened their doors to the Ukrainians.

I was watching what was happening with anxiety and concern as, after all, every day some of my relatives or friends made a decision to emigrate. Should we settle in another part of Ukraine or should we go as far from the war as possible? That question troubled many refugees. Of course, we encouraged and supported one another in that difficult situation as best we could, but many still chose to leave the country. All that caused a great emotional pain.

Thus, the decision of my brother Oleksandr to emigrate was a heavy blow. It was only several days since we had evacuated together. My brother helped so much with that difficult journey. We had just begun to get settled in Ivano-Frankivsk and planned to continue together.

Oleksandr struggled greatly trying to decide whether to stay in Ukraine and help as a volunteer or to take his family abroad. He had underage children—a son and two daughters. Because of the war, men were not allowed to leave the country unless they had three or more children. My brother felt torn, so he asked for advice and considered all the pros and cons. I saw that it was very hard for his wife, Inna. She turned forty right before their departure. Our team decided to hold a little birthday celebration for her during breakfast. We bought a small cake, ordered pizza, sang a song, congratulated her, and prayed for her. Inna thanked us but said sadly as she tried to hold back her tears, "I could never imagine that I would be celebrating my fortieth birthday during the war as a refugee, far away from home!"

They planned to leave the next day. I learned about it the night before. As their departure was approaching, pain and sadness filled my heart. Our whole family came to the church on March 3. As soon as I greeted the people who had come to have breakfast in the cafeteria, my brother arrived. Our families met in the yard between the church building and a three-story addition to it. The space was used as a parking lot. That morning it was half empty, so our families had a chance to say our good-byes in private. That parking lot had already witnessed many heartbreaking partings. Later, I often heard that people tried to avoid that place, because it reminded them of the times when they said good-bye to those who despaired and chose emigration. What looked like a regular parking lot to the inhabitants of Ivano-Frankivsk, for the refugees from Kherson and other locations became a sort of "Weeping Wall" with its painful reminder of the losses Israel had had to face in her time. Every day that parking lot witnessed the "loss" of our relatives and friends.

Oleksandr and his wife looked upset. It was obvious that the decision to leave was a hard one. As for their children, Nikita and Kira tried to be brave, but Angela, the second daughter, was crying bitterly. We hugged each other. I noticed that the morning was gloomy, as if Nature herself could not bear those incessant partings of the refugees and had covered the sky with dark clouds that were ready to cry rain tears.

"We must hurry." Oleksandr's voice was cracking. "Need to leave in twenty minutes."

It was frightening to think that there was no knowing when I would see and hug my brother again. Our lives had been intertwined for fifteen years. We were neighbors and shared a backyard. Never had a quarrel. Our families always celebrated Christmas and New Year together. And now we had only twenty measly minutes to say good-bye. It was a great shock to me, and I could see that Oleksandr felt the same.

"Valentyn, I am leaving our old VW with you," said my brother at the parting. "I would like to serve people in this way, at least. You can use it for evacuation."

We prayed and hugged. Then we parted.

The checkpoints at the border were overcrowded. The journey was undertaken with great difficulty. Oleksandr left for the Czech Republic, and from there—for the USA. Even now, after some time has passed, I still miss my brother, his openness, his sense of humor, and the long conversations held in my house as we were drinking coffee.

That parting showed another aspect of the war—it deprives you of hugs, steals touches of the people who are incredibly dear to you. But then it helps you value those who stay with you even more—family, friends, coworkers, and, of course, the church.

The next Sunday, March 6, we were glad to be at the church again where people greeted one another with the words "Praise to the Lord!" It is just amazing that in this part of the country you will not hear habitual "hello" or "greetings" at the church. The Christians of Ivano-Frankivsk believe that the only proper way to greet one another is to say "Praise to the Lord!" It is important to respond with the words "Eternal praise!" If you say anything else, you can be mistaken for a nonbeliever or a Jehovah's Witness. It is not very clear to the people from Kherson why the name of God has to be a part of the greeting. When we heard it for the first time, it almost sounded like using the name of the Lord in vain.

The church was crowded. The reason was the same as the last time—the influx of refugees from all over Ukraine. The pastor was even thinking of adding another worship service. Because several Kherson families had emigrated, our ranks had noticeably thinned. We took places on the ground floor, and some of our young people who seemed to have already adapted went to sit in the balcony.

Many Protestant churches in Ukraine hold communion on the first Sunday of the month, which happened to be that day. I know how the evangelical congregations view the role of this sacrament and how it is performed at the worship service. But it was for the first time that I partook of the Lord's Supper in Ivano-Frankivsk. It seemed to begin as it would at any other Baptist church in Ukraine. First, we sang, and the pastor preached. Then the church sang a hymn about the redeeming suffering of the Lord. Serhiy, the senior pastor, read a passage from Scripture that prompted us to think about that Passover meal when Christ offered to his disciples bread and wine as symbols of his suffering for the first time.

"If you are at peace with the Lord and the people," the pastor called, "you can partake of the communion with us."

The way the rest of the communion service was held reminded me of the Catholic Church. The pastor prayed for the bread lying on the gilded plate on the table and passed it on to his helpers. They began to walk slowly around the hall, putting pieces of bread into the hands of the believers. In Kherson, we are used to sending the plates with bread along the rows and having people pick up pieces themselves. The same is done with the trays with wine. But here, after the blessing of the pastor, the helpers took the wine to the people and served it to each one personally. The difference seemed to be insignificant, yet it indicated the importance for every Christian to partake of the communion through the ministry of a minister.

One day I happened to visit Salzburg, Mozart's hometown, in Austria. I walked around the city and then went to the Catholic cathedral. Besides admiring the architecture, I was able to observe the ritual of the Eucharist. I noticed something that separated the clergy from the parishioners. Raised on the biblical doctrine of the priesthood of all believers, I felt a little uncomfortable in that church. The role of the Reformation became clearer to me: Luther and Calvin had helped the believers overcome the centuries-long boundaries and become open to new experience. It was Martin Luther who was a pioneer in many ways. For example, he was not afraid to experiment with folk music and adapt it to the worship of God. He considered music to be second only to theology. It is no accident that in the following eras the church was blessed with many great musicians like

Bach, Beethoven, Haydn, and Mozart. It seems to be just one small touch, but it changed many things on the canvas of history, and that was all because of the Reformation.

The communion at the church in Ivano-Frankivsk ended with the copastors of Serhiy returning after serving the people and taking communion from the hands of the senior pastor. He was the last one to partake of the Lord's Supper, as he held the highest church office. The worship service ended with a special prayer.

I looked around. There were about a hundred believers in the church. Judging by their happy faces, they were used to that model of communion. It would have been wrong to devalue the significance of that worship service; after all, the people found the Lord in it, which was the most important thing! Looking into the eyes of our brothers and sisters, I realized how much they had already done for us refugees during the last several days. I was grateful for their hospitality. Even though we had many dissimilarities, it was best to look for that which encouraged unity. We could concentrate not on the difference in the ways to do communion but on the open arms with which God welcomes each of us. And no matter how anyone views life and traditions, the Lord accepts us all, and he expects us to do the same.

Acceptance is not a simple or onetime action in the relationships between the people. It rarely brings comfort to those who show it. Some cost is involved. Especially if both sides intend to cooperate successfully for a long time. Good relationships require efforts. This calls for the analogy with the process of the development of a pearl in the mollusk. When a grain of sand gets inside the shell, it causes pain and discomfort. It is like having a pebble in the shoe, of which we hasten to get rid. But the mollusk cannot do that, so it does something else. To get relief from suffering, it envelops the foreign element with special liquid. And it repeats the process again and again until it adapts to an annoying cohabitant and turns the latter into a glimmering pearl.

I think that this is how our forced move from Kherson to Ivano-Frankivsk should be viewed. This whole situation is the process of giving birth to "pearls," that is, relationships inside the evangelical church and with the inhabitants of western Ukraine. You cannot just get rid of the pebble: Christian principles, Ukrainian citizenship, invasion—all these factors have produced circumstances that make us all work on the relationships together. There is no doubt that the locals had already sacrificed some things to accommodate us. Now it was our turn to accept them, to strive for harmony, and to strengthen fragile peace.

The same day, my wife and I were unexpectedly invited to dinner. Yaroslav Kibit, one of the deacons in the church, had already been a great blessing to our family by offering us his three-room apartment to stay in. And now he was showing us heartfelt hospitality. His wife and daughters lovingly prepared a feast. I was very glad that Pastor Serhiy and his wife were also invited to dinner. That unforgettable evening encouraged our deep and close relationship. We talked on various pastoral topics enthusiastically and without reserve. We swapped stories from our life and ministries. Two hours simply flew by.

The unexpected climax of the evening was an invitation to preach at the local church! I was surprised. I hardly knew them, and yet I was already entrusted with preaching on the Epistle to the Romans. I understood that it was not easy for a church accustomed to its own ways to accept a minister from a different background, and still, they were willing to do it.

How do I view it? As a clear manifestation of respect and honor, a confirmation that I am now a part of the church, that I belong!

Chapter 5

Kherson Occupied

SOMEBODY APTLY NOTED THAT REGARDLESS of where Ukrainians were when the war began—whether in Kharkiv, Kyiv, Sumy, Chernihiv, or Kherson—each of them thinks February 24 to be the longest of days. Some could not help feeling paralyzed by the unexpectedness of the events, and even though they had a chance to move to a safer place, they were immobilized by fear. Others evacuated without any hesitation, but finding themselves far from home, they discovered that their hearts remained in their homeland. I know by experience what it means to be a displaced person. Each of us is like an uprooted tree replanted in new soil. Everything keeps reminding us of the place from which our roots have been removed.

We lived in Ivano-Frankivsk, over five hundred miles away from home, yet our thoughts were with Kherson. There was not so much nostalgia as anxiety in our hearts: How are our relatives, friends, neighbors, houses, towns, and villages? All that worried us and occupied our thoughts as we were far away. We were greatly pained to hear daily news about air attacks, shelling, and the landing of Russian troops in the suburbs of Kherson. The enemy was approaching steadily. Numerous videos on the Internet confirmed the occupation of the town of Oleshky, located just across the river from Kherson. It was hard to watch the recordings of fierce battles for Antonivka Bridge: monstrous explosions, piles of burnt military vehicles, asphalt cut by tanks' tracks. Soon we began getting not-so-good news from our relatives and friends that the city was besieged, roads around it taken, and the villages of Antonivka, Zelenivka, and Chornobaivka occupied. Yet Russians did not enter Kherson for several days. They were seen in the suburbs. But many convoys of military vehicles with white Z-signs went across the bridge in the direction of Mykolaiv.

Even those ignorant of war would understand that Kherson was under siege, and the enemy continued to move deeper into the country.

When the war is over, we may find out why the south of Ukraine was not properly protected against the invasion. How did it happen? Why was the enemy able to come from Crimea if the territory at the border was supposed to have been mined? Why were neither irrigation pipes made into a natural obstacle nor bridges blown up to prevent the advance of military vehicles? The whole story smells of treason, especially when we remember that right before the war military drills of the Ukrainian army were carried out in the south of Ukraine. Yet a month later, Russian troops moved deep into the Kherson region and got hold of strategic objects like Kakhovka Dam and Antonivka Bridge, which opened the door to the key cities of Kherson, Mykolaiv, and Odesa.

Those of us who stayed in Ivano-Frankivsk watched the news closely. We called the people in Kherson as often as possible. At that time, all the Ukrainian territories occupied by Russia still got the service of Ukrainian mobile providers. It was Oleh Derkachenko who informed us of what was happening to TCI. His house was close to Antonivka Bridge and the TCI campus. Oleh did not want to evacuate because of his family and pastoral responsibility to the church. He visited the TCI campus daily and told us what was going on. We have known Oleh for a long time. You would have never guessed that he had a wild, sinful past. When he was a little child, he lost his leg playing recklessly on the railroad tracks. Wild behavior in his youth caused him to become a drug addict. The vile addiction almost got him imprisoned, which, in its turn, prompted him to turn to God. He became an amazing person: a father of eight children, pastor of a church in Antonivka. He worked as the academic dean at TCI for several years. Right before the war, he made a decision to leave that post because of the workload at the church, but he still continued to teach theological subjects at the Institute. He loved playing soccer, and not many people could guess that he had an artificial leg.

In our absence, Oleh looked after TCI staff remaining at the campus who took care of the garden, maintenance of the facilities, and guarding of the campus. They were mostly men in their fifties and sixties. Some of them had been broken by the addiction to alcohol, caused by divorce or other difficult circumstances. After their rehabilitation, they joined one of the churches of Kherson and tried to reenter the society, earning its trust. TCI provided them with jobs, housing, and food. Some pastors would visit them from time to time and serve them. Then Oleh became their mentor.

There were also cooks and cleaners working at TCI. There was a gardener, an elderly man, who lived close to the campus. They were all residents of Antonivka, in which TCI was located. Some of them were evangelicals; others called themselves Orthodox.

The first days of March were darkened by the news that Russians began to storm the city. The enemy shelled private houses of the residents, then small groups of soldiers were seen in the streets. Military transport entered the city. The locals testified that Z-marked vehicles of the enemy came in a cowardly manner, as if in fear. People said that the mayor rejected a proposition of the Russian commander to establish the military administration in Kherson. People were furious. They were ready to snap and attack the occupants. Some understood that it was useless to go against an armed enemy without weapons and began looking for ways to move to safer places. But for many, it was impossible to evacuate their families. The only thing left for them was to accept things as they were and hope for liberation. People were getting used to occupation. Although it is hardly possible to get used to the thought that the enemy has captured your country and that his actions are unpredictable—the occupants did act ruthlessly.

We heard scary stories of what was going on in Chornobaivka. Russians acted cruelly there. They entered the houses of civilians, threatened them, and killed them. In the outskirts of the village, soldiers fired heavy machine guns at cars filled with people going to Mykolaiv. About thirty dead bodies were lying at the side of the road for several days. Nobody dared to approach them. Finally, three priests decided to go, hold a death Mass, and bury the deceased. I knew one of the priests, Serhiy Deinekin, very well.

Serhiy used to be a helicopter pilot, then he built houses using Canadian technology while pastoring a church. He studied at TCI, but in the beginning of the war he had to take an academic leave. I recall warmly the pastoral meetings held at his church and the delicious dumplings with which he and his wife treated the ministers. His spouse was a very nice and open lady. She could always surprise you with some new fashion trends. She liked to show off a new blouse or new shoes simply and good-naturedly. Serhiy was a kindly man, and his red hair and freckles always endeared people to him. Many in the area were surprised at his close friendship with Greek Catholic and Orthodox priests. Sometimes it was hard to imagine that there was a part of the world where representatives of different Christian denominations could have such intimate fellowship. Locals often saw the ministers from those three confessions holding spiritual meetings at which they sang Christian songs together. Those were the ministers who had to bury the people killed near Chornobaivka in those evil days.

It is hard to imagine what those three ministers had to go through. It was not without consequences. Serhiy Deinekin was arrested by the occupants. They kept him for an entire day, intimidating and threatening him. Later the other two priests had to leave the village because Russians would not leave them alone. But Serhiy stayed in Chornobaivka.

Many ministers in Kherson were connected with TCI in one way or another. Some studied at the Institute, others taught there, yet others acted as board members. I and my colleagues were friends with many of them, so we knew all about the hard work the Christians in Kherson did during the occupation. It told us much about the decisive role the believers played there at that time.

Despite all the difficulties, evangelical churches became aid centers, because pastors, ministers, and common Christians felt the pain of the people acutely and rushed to help. The houses of prayer were made into bomb shelters and soup kitchens. We heard that Golgotha Baptist Church in Kherson took in little children from the local orphanage. Children from one to five years of age stayed in the basement of the church together with medical personnel and caretakers because Russians hunted for children, took them, and sent them to Russia. It is one of the blackest pages in the history of Ukraine, and it was the churches that were some of the first to step up to protect children.

Disaster united people. Christians readily responded to what was going on. Church members worked as volunteers supporting residents, doing good to them, evacuating them. War forced some believers to take responsibility they had not had before. A good example of this is the case of Oleh Volontyrtsev from Ostriv Church (a Christian congregation in one of the suburbs of Kherson called "Ostriv").

For as long as I knew Oleh before the war, he was always in charge of sound and lighting equipment at his church. He was a good expert who was often asked to help with technical support at the special events in the city in which popular stars took part. Despite his professionalism, he never changed as a person. He was always unpretentious, helpful, and sometimes even shy. It was nice to see his six-foot-tall figure towering over the mixing console in the worship hall. Oleh was about fifty. He was incredibly kind and quiet, but if someone was able to get him talking, he would start to joke. I remember how one time he was laughing at himself, saying, "If I had two sons, they would have been called Chuk and Gek!"*

Ostriv Church remained without pastors—they and their families got evacuated during the first days of the invasion. Oleh Volontyrtsev stepped up to support the congregation. He preached, distributed humanitarian aid, organized volunteers. Thus, gradually, he got involved in the ministry usually perceived as pastoral. Oleh's experience is not unique. We have heard many stories of church members, for example, businessmen, who had to become ministers.

* Chuk and Gek are characters from a children's book popular in Soviet times.

It was wonderful that churches stayed strong thanks to such people and became support centers for the population.

We watched the situation in Kherson closely. There was a shortage of food and medicine in the city because Russians blocked the deliveries from the Ukrainian side, and the aid from Russia was becoming much more limited. There were lengthy negotiations between Ukrainian and Russian authorities regarding the establishment of a humanitarian corridor to allow civilians to leave the city and bring in food, drinking water, and medicine. People sometimes had to stand in line for hours to buy food. We wanted to help. Since there were many food items stored for students at TCI's storehouses, we asked one of our workers who had been responsible for construction at the campus to be in charge of the food, to cook, and to feed TCI personnel and residents of Antonivka. TCI also had hothouses in which cucumbers and radishes had been grown for several years. That year we did not plant radishes, but in March we harvested cucumbers. We were able to sell just a small portion of them; the rest was distributed among the needy.

War affected the economy of our region greatly; after all, our area is agricultural. In Velyki Kopani, a village about forty minutes away from Kherson, there was a big all-Ukrainian vegetable market. Because of the war activities in the region, it was inactive for a long time. Farmers suffered great losses. Witnesses reported that tons of radishes were dumped at the side of the road or in the forest belts. It was not only farmers who suffered losses. A poultry farm in Chornobaivka, one of the biggest and most modern ventures to produce eggs in Europe, lost electricity because of the shelling. Fodder could not be brought in time because of the delays at checkpoints. Hens were dying. The stench of decay could be smelled for miles around the place. All that could result in a global ecological catastrophe. It was impossible to sell all the eggs and hens fast since there were too many of them. They were given away to the people, but it did not help much. The farm suffered losses. These are just two examples, but there were also many big enterprises plus countless small businesses in the war-torn region. It will take a long time to heal all the wounds inflicted by the war.

An alarming signal coming on March 10 from Kherson made us worry.

"The guests came," Oleh Derkachenko informed us on the phone. "Two Russian soldiers walked around the campus, inspected all the buildings, took pictures of everything. They are gone."

"What did they want?" I asked.

We felt that a visit of such "guests" did not bode well. We were right. On the next day, March 11, a Russian Z-marked convoy came to the gates of TCI. Two hundred machine gunners. There were women among them. Suddenly the TCI campus became a military base. Soldiers settled in our buildings freely and started acting like owners. In the beginning, they did not bother our guards and let the latter keep watch at the gates and look after the campus. But the rest of the workers were not allowed in anymore.

We were trying to figure out why the Russians needed TCI. There was only one answer: the campus was a convenient place for a military installation since it was situated between Antonivka Bridge and the railroad bridge the military had to control. It looked like the "guests" had come to stay. They brought a stolen generator to be independent of the electricity provided by the city, because there were power outages at that time. Neighbors also said that the Russians set up a mobile crematory. It was unclear what was going on there, but a fetid stench hung over the TCI campus from time to time.

Meanwhile, there were rumors in the city that Russia was going to hold a referendum in order to create "a people's republic" in Kherson like they did in the Donetsk and Luhansk regions. A Ukrainian flag still flew at city hall, but the situation was getting worse and worse. Residents began to hold demonstrations against the occupation. There were many videos on the Internet showing the inhabitants of Kherson shouting in unison, "Go home! Go home!" and "Russian soldier is a Nazi and occupant!"

At first, the demonstrators were not harmed, but then soldiers began to disperse them using stun grenades and shooting in the air. Our acquaintances told us that the occupational regime started to stage demonstrations in support of Russia throughout the entire region. Here is a story I heard from one of my friends, Pastor Yevhen Bondarenko from Nova Kakhovka.

In March, Russian soldiers burst into the building rented by the church during a Sunday worship service. They broke the door and alarm system. They were trying to stop the worship service claiming that they had received information about a demonstration to be held there. Five sharpshooters went to the roof to control the territory from above.

Pastor Bondarenko honestly admitted that it was hard to continue with the worship service because the worshipers were scared. It is hard to imagine being surrounded by armed people whose actions cannot be predicted. One feels like Daniel the prophet in the lions' den. It is impossible to foresee what these wild animals are going to do. Still, the believers calmed down, and the worship service continued. But what happened next made it clear that the occupants had planned the demonstration for a while.

"Fifteen vans with civilians came," Yevhen reported. "There were about forty people holding Russian flags. They tried to look like locals. There were also some cameramen. An armored car with soldiers was there as well. Then a demonstration began. Somebody was using a loudspeaker." At the same time, it was expected that as the believers left the worship service, they would have to get mixed with the crowd. A man dressed as a civilian came in and proposed to those present to join the demonstration. Nobody moved. One lady mustered her courage and shouted, "We need neither you nor your 'Russian world'!" It seemed that the man did not expect such an answer. He moved angrily, betraying that he was rather a member of special services and not a civilian. He had to leave the room embarrassed.

Thus, the church involuntarily witnessed the staging of a demonstration in support of Russia to which fake Ukrainians were brought.

As for Kherson, it was becoming more and more unsafe in the city. Russian soldiers filled the streets. Their presence frightened local girls and women. Afraid of being captured by the occupants and raped, women feared even leaving their homes. If they had to go out, they tried to dress unassumingly. People were kidnapped often. Not only governmental workers or city activists who refused to cooperate with Russian military men but also common inhabitants. Phone chats were "pulsing" with the pain of residents: hundreds of people were losing contact with relatives and friends—people kept disappearing. I remember being stung by the news that a son of Oleksandr Babiychuk, the director of the Ukrainian Bible Society, was kidnapped. Kherson was constantly stunned by such cases. For example, one morning Serhiy Chudinovich, the priest of Holy Mother of God Church, a well-known city activist and volunteer, was arrested in his own church.

On top of that, searches were conducted everywhere. There were several reasons for that. First of all, Russians were afraid that partisan groups could appear. Second, many Russian soldiers deserted. They were young men who, finding themselves in Ukraine, refused to fight and ran away. Russians looked for them in abandoned buildings and churches. Apparently, Russians assumed that the believers would not refuse to help fugitives out of kindness. The Russians paid special attention to the buildings that belonged to the "Baptists" (the occupants applied the term "Baptist" to all the evangelical Protestant churches). During one of those raids, Russians came to the Church of Christ the Savior, pastored by my father, Serhiy Syniy.

"That day all the streets leading to the church were suddenly blocked by armored cars," my father told me. "A huge tank stood before the entrance pointing its barrel at the building. It was a frightening sight, as if we were some kind of terrorists. All around the church stood machine gunners, so that nobody could escape. The raid began."

The soldiers searched the entire building, looking into every nook and cranny. In the basement, they found some medicine and interrogated my father about that for a long time. He was accused of helping partisans and threatened.

We were not surprised at the Russians' attitude toward Protestant churches. We could see the way they treated TCI. When Russian soldiers settled in our buildings, Leonid Matseyka, a vice president, got a call from a Russian officer. The latter listed some of the items that belonged to TCI, including a sewage truck, and impudently proposed that TCI administration buy them from him. It did not take us long to refuse the offer from the racketeer. In the very beginning of the war, all our ministers agreed that we would never negotiate with Russians. Our refusal made the officer mad.

"You are Nazis, fascists, and American spies!" he yelled at Leonid. "You are sectarians, and if we had caught you here, we would have buried you alive! Know that there will be only one true church—the Russian Orthodox Church—here!"

That unpleasant call revealed another terrible aspect of the war—pillage, robbery, and marauding. Victor Hugo, a French novelist, wrote in *Les Miserables* that each army has a tail of marauders attached to it. The impudent racketeering of the Russian officer tells me something about the discipline in the modern Russian army. If high-ranking officers did not shy away from robbery on a larger scale, the virus of pillaging was sure to affect their subordinates. It starts with begging for food from the locals, then the appetite of the soldiers grows considerably and turns them into impudent marauders just like their commanders. Hugo called it legitimized robbery. Residents of Kherson suffered from that. Robbery did not spare TCI.

Two weeks after the soldiers had settled in at the TCI campus, a rotation seemed to take place and a new group came. Some say they were "Kadyrovtsy."* It was unbearable for the remaining TCI staff to live in such proximity to them. The first group of soldiers was at least trying to pretend that they were not occupants, but now the military men abandoned every pretense. They threw our guards out, warning them, "If you show up here again, we will shoot you!" Then they began to steal valuable items. They took plasma TVs and

* "Kadyrovtsy" refers to a military unit under the command of Ramzan Kadyrov, the president of Chechnya. The term is often associated with extreme brutality.

projectors from the auditoriums and orthopedic mattresses from the bedrooms. They stole kitchenware. We heard outrageous stories of Russian soldiers inviting prostitutes to our campus and paying for their services with dishes from the Institute's dining hall.

The library was one of the "pearls" of TCI. It contained a great number of theological and devotional books. Many of these treasures were bought with donations from our partners. The aggressors destroyed all the books in Ukrainian and English as "foreign" and "Nazi."

How painful is this feeling of helplessness you get when you hear news from Kherson! You feel impotent since you cannot do anything about it. You are incapable of stopping the raging evil. Sometimes it seems to be some kind of cruel and unusual punishment: to watch silently as everything that you used to live for, that you liked, that made you and many others happy sinking into oblivion. It is so unfair that it takes such a short time for a war to obliterate the fruit of hard work of many years.

Yes, we were in Ivano-Frankivsk, a relatively safe place, but we were all perturbed by the news from the south. Refugees are familiar with the feeling of shame, this little "bonus" of war: you live far away from the front line and can make small plans, for example, to take a walk, while the bombs are destroying Kherson, your Kherson. The city where your heart still is. You are pained by the thoughts of Kherson and ashamed of your safety. You wish the day would come when evil would be stopped. But until then you can only sigh together with millions of Ukrainians and try to find strength to help your country and your people.

Chapter 6

Turning Point

I REMEMBER HOW WE LEFT KHERSON on February 24, the first day of the war. Despite all our preparations for a possible evacuation, the suddenness of Russian invasion rendered us powerless. Strong emotions were boiling inside me, and I could not calm down. It seemed reasonable to give in to anxious thoughts. I was preoccupied with the thought that as a man, I should step up and defend my motherland instead of evacuating with the rest of the team. I rushed to get it off my chest: "Luba, what if we get the people to the west of Ukraine, and then I return to Kherson?"

It was somewhat difficult to articulate that. I noticed several times that my wife was stealthily weeping, sitting in the passenger seat next to me.

"Valik, what are you going to do there?"

I breathed out. The steppes of Kherson stretched outside the window. The convoy of cars was moving slowly. The decision suddenly made demanded an immediate action.

"I will join TDF (Territorial Defense forces)!"

Articulating my decision, I realized that it was the maximum that I could do as the president of a Christian institute. Although my father served in the missile forces, I was raised on the principles of pacifism.

"I will not oppose it," Luba said.

My wife's father was in the military. She knew by experience what a life in the army was like, so she could see me joining TDF.

We were silent for a while. I was thinking how I was always sure of the importance of the pastoral calling. I have often taught young ministers that pastoral ministry is above all other occupations, because a pastor is able to make an impact on the eternal destiny of a person. Of course, all the professions are good and important, but their influence is not so lasting.

But a war comes, and the reality changes immediately. You think nothing will make you rethink your life, but suddenly you find yourself facing a question, "What do I do?" The time is short. Reason is bombarded with oppressive thoughts. All the alternatives rush through your head. And each individual who faces the war has to deal with his or her personal challenges.

"How effectively does pastoral ministry meet the needs of the people in crisis?" I reflected, trying to understand myself and my feelings. "Do I need to leave the ministry inside the church and stay close to my suffering people as much as I can? Can the fight on the front line be the mission of a good Christian?"

At that moment, fear seemed to disappear. Instead, I felt anger rising inside me. It prompted me to immediate action. I wanted to hit the wheel in order to let, at least, some emotions out.

Suddenly I remembered the instructions of Ethan Norton, our safety consultant. He taught that during a war, those who make rash decisions are the first to die. Yes, of course, many people acted worthily and even heroically in the current situation. But they did not assess the risks. To be a military man is also a calling that requires professional skills that help carry this burden with confidence. War does not spare those who act rashly, giving in to their emotions, without even understanding the necessity to be prepared.

Reflecting on Ethan's recommendations, I kept asking myself, "How can I help my people in this time most effectively?"

Now there seemed to be no prospects for me. Only the unchanging canvas of the road, a convoy of cars, and the monotonous Kherson steppe. I talked to my wife and children from time to time and answered the phone. Suddenly Taras Dyatlik, my old acquaintance, called me. I remembered it was today that we were to take part in a TCI strategic planning meeting (a project to maintain the vitality of an educational institution) in Chisinau, Moldova. I had to postpone the journey because of the situation in the country.

CHAPTER 6

"Hi, Valentyn."

Our friendship with Taras began in the autumn of 2007 at a conference in Irpin. At that time, we were young leaders: I had been TCI president for just about a year, and he was the academic dean of Donetsk Christian University. That encouraged our friendship. When Russians invaded the Donetsk region in 2014, Taras moved to work at Euro-Asian Accrediting Association (EAAA), which was involved in developing partnerships and educational standards in former Soviet republics. It united about fifty educational institutions, including TCI.

"I am returning from Chisinau to Rivne now," Taras began to tell me when he found out that I and other TCI staff had already left Kherson. "You cannot imagine, Valentyn, how many cars are going from Ukraine to Moldova now."

"Taras," I interrupted, "I do not need to imagine. I am now a part of one such convoy. There are many cars and many traffic jams on the roads. People are running away from the war."

"I understand. You know, Valentyn, I feel a little strange. I seem to be the only one driving to Ukraine now. So I am reflecting on what I am going to do there. After all, you and I are in theological education, and all we can do on the front line is to jump out of the trench carrying the flag and shouting, 'Long live Ukraine!'"

I could picture it very well. Taras was always good at making people laugh. Now was not a time for joking, but he was right: our abilities to serve at the front were incredibly limited. My wife and I had been discussing something similar minutes earlier.

"Our professional skills may not be the ones most needed at the front," Taras continued optimistically on the phone. "Still, I believe we can organize the work on the home front."

"What do you suggest?" I was falling under the spell of his train of thought.

"Well, we can create a network of like-minded people and begin to help Ukrainians effectively in the time of war."

Our rapid-paced conversation led us to the conclusion that the war demanded new initiatives from us, and seminaries needed to switch to the ministry related to humanitarian aid. We needed to help refugees in many ways. Despite the distance and circumstances, Taras and I began to earnestly discuss a fund that would support the theological education in Ukraine. It was exciting to do the brainstorming and formulate possible strategic questions of the future work right there at the wheel.

"Then let's stay in touch, Valentyn," Taras concluded. "Take care of yourself!"

I could hear only the monotonous noise of car motors. The drab landscape of the Kherson steppe still stretched outside the window. The line of vehicles seemed endless. Nothing changed. Yet something momentous had already wound its way into my heart. My conversation with Taras struck a special spark, set the wood that had long lain inside me on fire. I remembered that already in December 2021 I got an offer to leave the country to use my skills to work with partners. But I chose to stay with TCI. Now, as we were leaving Kherson, the call of Taras alleviated my anguish as to what I was going to do and how I could employ my abilities. I discovered an area in which I could work well.

Although Taras and I were still on the road, we began to act immediately. We established a group in Telegram and started making calls, getting some people of influence in that area involved. We began reflecting on how we could help seminaries raise funds for common projects and develop partnerships effectively. That was how Refugee Fund was established. Besides Taras, it included Roman Soloviy, Taras's sister Olha Dyatlik (Overseas Council–United World Mission), bookkeeper Kateryna Shunko, and three seminary presidents: me (TCI), Oleksandr Geychenko (Odesa Seminary), and Ivan Rusyn (Ukrainian Theological Seminary). Evan Hunter (Scholar Leaders) and Scott Cunningen (Overseas Council–United World Mission) stayed in touch with us all the time.

It was also the time when the idea of a TCI fund to support displaced people was born. It was supposed to involve all the key partners of our institute. By the end of our journey from Kherson to Ivano-Frankivsk, we already had a clear understanding of the purpose of the fund: to help refugees and churches suffering from the hardships caused by the war. The flywheel of the ministry began to spin. We were still on the road, yet our partner church in Colorado was already receiving funds to help the refugees from the US churches.

I can't say that it was all done knowingly. I was burdened by the war just like any other Ukrainian. And just like any of them, I put all my energy into rescuing my family on that fateful day. As a result, I got a great emotional burden and a ticket to the unknown. The overloaded highway from Kherson to Mykolaiv could hardly accommodate thousands of refugees' cars. It is amazing that at the time, I had strength to think not only of myself but also of helping others. Maybe that was why the opportunities seemed to come up without me trying to find them. During the entire journey to Ivano-Frankivsk, representatives of various organizations contacted me to say some words of encouragement. I heard many assurances of people's willingness to help. All that meant a lot in that difficult situation.

I remember the calls from IDES (International Disaster Emergency Service), which made one of the first donations to help refugees and facilitate evacuation. I remember the call from Read Ministry. PBT also contacted me to get information on their workers whom TCI helped evacuate. I will never forget how touched I was by the sincere compassion and support of the journalists of *Christian Standard*. I also recall long conversations with *Christianity Today*: they could not believe that Russians invaded Ukraine and kept asking me the same question over and over again.

Some phone calls were disturbing. I had an odd conversation with a representative of an organization that was very stressed because of the war. They demanded that we return the money they had allotted to TCI for one of the educational projects before the war.

"We need this money!"

"But we are on the road right now, getting evacuated . . . ," I replied.

"Give us the money back; we are not sure how your organization will fare during the war."

"We are not going to stop working. Please, just let us get to a safe place first."

"We can make no exceptions for you. We are not sure now if TCI can carry out the project to which the money has been allotted. Give us the money back. In cash."

"May we, at least, transfer the money to your bank account? We are on the road, as I said, and it is impossible to get cash at the moment."

"We do not need a bank transfer, only cash!"

The conversation left an impression that some people had no sensitivity or understanding of the situation in which the whole country found itself. Of course, later the representatives of that organization apologized for their faintheartedness, but at that fateful moment, the conversation hit me hard, which was the last thing I needed in a crisis situation when one stress was added to another.

Sometimes I think that all that has been happening in Ukraine has been a litmus test that clearly shows people's attitudes. It is understood that the suddenness of the war left many people paralyzed. I could feel it when I would call my acquaintances asking for help and get cold refusals. The most encouraging thing that I heard was "I am going to pray for you." It was encouraging, but, at the same time, I detected fearfulness in the voices of the people, as if they had a hard time pronouncing that phrase.

Yes, those were unseemly aspects of one and the same phenomenon—war. It would be wrong to judge the people who gave in to fear. I believe that they should be shown grace and forgiveness, and we ought to be glad that such conversations at the time were few compared to the many calls of encouragement. After all, a great number of individuals and organizations all around the world understood the situation and rushed to help the Ukrainians. One of them was Hans, my friend from Holland.

The call of Hans Hamoen came during our evacuation. He asked about what was going on and suddenly proposed to send some potatoes to the churches in the Kherson region through TCI (later, it turned out that the first truck contained twenty tons of potatoes).

I told him I was on the road and not sure whether someone in Kherson could undertake the project, considering all the commotion going on there. But Hans was persuasive, and I promised to do something about it.

We had been friends with Hans for eight years. In 2014, I attended a conference dedicated to the ministry in Central Asia. It was a difficult time for TCI. One of the important sources of revenue for us was the money we got from hiring out the TCI campus for summer camps, conferences, and weddings. After the annexation of Crimea, most of the organizations that had rented our facilities began to look for other places for their events. Since Kherson was close to occupied Crimea, they were concerned about the safety of the participants. The income of the Institute dropped considerably. Though just two years earlier our campus had been rented every summer, it was now an undesirable location to hold events. Our board recommended looking for new opportunities for self-financing.

A minister we knew suggested that we invest in a hothouse and grow cucumbers. It just so happened that while at that conference, I saw a seminar entitled "Business as Mission" on the schedule. There I met speakers from New Zealand, Germany, Finland, Canada, and the USA. But it was Hans from Holland with whom we became friends. Hans Hamoen was involved in farming, among other things, and I knew that the Dutch were famous for the high quality of their agricultural produce. I asked Hans to consult with us as we were beginning our new enterprise. The south of Ukraine was not a part of his missionary vision, but he gladly shared his experience with hothouses.

Since then, we would meet every spring and talk about business. He also told me about his personal life, his children and his wife, who could not travel with him because of her back problems. Thus, a genuine and simple friendship between Hans and me developed. We were not involved in common projects, and he did not make any donations to TCI. We were just friends. This was the first time that he suggested we do a humanitarian project together.

When I came to Ivano-Frankivsk, I got in touch with the pastors closely connected with farming in the south of Ukraine. "Valentyn," they told me, "thank you, but there is war going on for several days already, and potatoes are difficult to store. Canned food would be better."

I passed on their answer to Hans. He heard me out and said that if we needed help, his organization would be happy to provide it. I thanked my friend for his kindness. But I continued to reflect on his proposition. There are several principles that I am guided by in my life: never give up and help my friends. So, I kept calling my acquaintances until I got a businessman from Mykolaiv excited about the project and willing to let us use his storehouse. During the long months of the occupation, that storehouse served as a humanitarian hub for aid for the residents of Kherson and Mykolaiv.

You never know how significant an idea is until you implement it. I have often heard Americans say that baby steps are the key to success. It made sense to me after the call from Hans. Who would have thought that his request to help send potatoes to Kherson would become as momentous as the conversation with Taras Dyatlik? Every baby step TCI made opened a horizon of important projects. We had to accept the challenge, roll up our sleeves, and begin helping our country.

But one cannot do all this work alone. The years of my presidency at TCI showed me the advantage of partnerships. I have seen many proofs of their effectiveness. Individual efforts have limited success, but common work is a synergy that bears great fruit.

What can a little snowflake do, for example? What impact can it make? In those parts of the world where winters are snowy, people are familiar with the collapse of transportation when the roads get closed for days. And all because a little snowflake joins another, and they both merge with a bunch of other snowflakes, making a thick cover. Thus, the important arteries of roads get paralyzed. I understand that a partnership has a similar effect. And now, as we were facing the war and the scale of the tragedy was immeasurable, the strength of partnerships was relevant as never before.

Not only did I always value partnerships, but I often heard from my friends that I was good at building them. If asked what my secret was, I would answer that it was friendship. I have believed ever since childhood that a friendship is much more important than material blessings, so I can say with confidence that close relationships make the work with partners more efficient. Now I can see that no friendly conversation over a cup of coffee at the conferences has remained unfruitful. Making friends and enjoying long relationships with wonderful people have produced partnerships. I notice how the hearts become united in order to serve and help during hard times. It is no longer a personal friendship, but the whole network of close relationships with the organizations is being built based on the harmonious communication between churches and volunteers. During the war, it is worth its weight in gold.

War always implies the intensification of the enemy's efforts. The enemy tries to build up his strength: collaborators and traitors multiply—but that is just one side of it. The history of mankind proves that a crisis is a time of unique opportunities. It brings kind and responsive individuals and organizations to the foreground.

No matter how hard the war made life for my country, I wanted to see how, despite all the evil, true friends would reveal themselves. I think that it was the evacuation from Kherson that became the turning point.

Chapter 7

If You Save One Life, You Save the World

"When my daughter-in-law and I left the occupied territory, our only desire was to see at least one Ukrainian soldier," our staff member Olha told us. "We were so happy when we did!"

These words reminded us how tired the residents of Kherson were of the presence of Russian "liberators" so that when they finally got out and dreamed to rest and feel protected, the sight of one Ukrainian soldier alone could help with that.

It was worth helping evacuate people just to hear those words!

Our life in Ivano-Frankivsk was not easy. We did not find ourselves in a peaceful haven that high waves did not reach. The war produced tsunamis every day and drove them to our shores with such a force that we could not expect gentle surf or softly foaming water at the beach. The Russian invasion kept every Ukrainian on his toes. Even if a refugee managed to forget for a moment those who remained in the occupied areas, phone calls and messages made him start as if from the pain caused by an inflamed nerve. Besides, news from the front kept reminding us of their pitiable fate. So as soon as we were done with the work on the third floor, where most of the refugees from Kherson settled, we began to organize evacuation from the south.

It may have looked like a spontaneous action. But, after the discussions with the executive team and TCI board during our first days in the west, the Institute had to shift the focus of its ministry. Because of the war, we decided to evacuate people, take care of the refugees, and, of course, help those who remained in the temporarily occupied areas. The first thing we did was to repair the van that almost did not get us to Ivano-Frankivsk. It was the white Mercedes Sprinter bought in Kherson on the first day of the war. Interestingly enough, while we were still on the road, a pastor from Florida told our story on local television and raised a part of the sum to reimburse us for the purchase of the van. Some partner organizations also contributed a part of the amount paid for the vehicle. Understanding that we would need more transportation, we decided to use TCI money to buy another van. It was the same model as the first one, only green.

We wanted to help. It may have been an emotional decision at first. We may have lacked necessary knowledge. But all that did not matter because we wanted to take people out of Kherson, and there seemed to be an unending line of them. The enemy was approaching Mykolaiv, and many refugees fled through that city. It was there where our first vans took people. Besides, volunteers made trips in their own cars. Each of these journeys was life-threatening. Even in time of peace, a driver should remember that a car is a potential source of danger, but the war increases this danger immeasurably. Unsafe places become more numerous—after all, this is war! We understood that we would have to "plunge" into the new experience, and we needed to be prepared to avoid mistakes. We were glad to have Ethan Norton to help us with a new enterprise again. He had consulted TCI regarding the evacuation plan before. Now his help with the training of volunteer drivers came in handy as well.

On May 1, Ethan convened a Zoom seminar to support Ukraine. Being a military man, he talked about necessary skills to help protect our drivers and keep the chances of accidents and deaths to a minimum. Other experts joined Ethan on Zoom, and their recommendations also served us well. But Ethan's involvement did not end there. He asked us to set up a meeting with the organizations and volunteers who helped evacuate people in order to do a special training for them. As soon as we could organize that seminar, Ethan came with several other instructors to do the teaching. He also brought twenty satellite phones with him. It was one of the first sets of expensive equipment that came to Ukraine since the beginning of the war. There were always problems with communication at the front, but satellite phones solved them and made the work of volunteers easier. TCI passed on Ethan's gift to humanitarian aid organizations involved in evacuation.

Those trainings were by invitation only, and we did not advertise them. Ethan and his team provided our volunteer drivers with much information. The trainers were very experienced. They taught everything, starting with what kind of clothes to wear to remain inconspicuous and ending with the way to rescue people in case of battles. They also explained how to bypass enemy checkpoints, talk with the representatives of the TDF, and go through Ukrainian checkpoints. Our drivers also took a tactical medicine course. They were taught to give first aid to the wounded and stop the bleeding with the help of a tourniquet (a modern hemostat with a small lever, indispensable in the field). Later we were able to buy many tourniquets in Israel and the USA so that each driver would have at least two of them: one on his shoulder and another on his waist.

The information was practical, and it helped us a lot. It explained the difficult job of a volunteer who takes people from the front to a safe place in his car. He must learn to transport both an individual and a group. Each situation is different. One should be as much prepared as he can be. His car should be fixed and he should have warm blankets, drinking water, and high-calorie food. We bought vacuum-packed hot dogs and nutritious bars in Germany for that.

Ethan's training helped expose our lack of professionalism. It was no surprise because most of our professors and other staff did not have much driving experience. Before the evacuation, I drove no more than three hours at a time (except for the forced "record" of nine-to-twelve hours during the first day of the war when we were leaving Kherson). I was a city driver: I drove to work in the morning and back home in the evening, always using the same route—that was the extent of my professional driving. Driven by the desire to help refugees, the volunteers put themselves at risk: they could get in trouble not only by going to dangerous places but also by ignoring some seemingly insignificant things. For example, sometimes a driver would go without sleep and rest for a long time, just grabbing a bite now and then instead of having real meals. Now that all was taken into account. The volunteers changed their habits to make their hard work more effective.

The number of our drivers kept growing. Other refugees joined the team. Soon we had twenty volunteers bringing people out of dangerous areas. Then we realized that it was crucial to have someone to coordinate the work of the drivers, stay in touch with them throughout the entire evacuation journey from point A to point B, and inform them of potential dangers (war is always unpredictable). It was Serhiy Bolotov who started to take care of control and logistics. Before the war, he was the vice director of one of the biggest printing houses in Kherson, which published one of the most popular local newspapers. Serhiy had sent his wife and daughter to Europe and remained in Ivano-Frankivsk. His wife used to attend one of the churches in Kherson for a long time, so Serhiy knew many people. He quickly befriended TCI volunteers and soon offered to help. That was how he became the "brain" of the evacuation.

He solved all the complications with a lot of professionalism. Thanks to him, a special tracker was installed in each car in the convoy (there were usually at least four cars in each convoy). TCI bought the trackers in Poland. The tracker helped monitor the movement of the convoy on the map in our office, where you could observe the evacuation route online. The trackers also showed the speed of the vehicles—we encouraged the drivers not to go too fast or take unnecessary risks, which could happen because each trip to the front was emotionally exhausting for a volunteer. Sometimes, when a driver came home after such a trip, he would feel a fit of strong and unexplainable anger. Some volunteers said they were ashamed that they had left their city. And each driver admitted at some point that he felt sad because of losing his home.

When I heard the feedback of the volunteers, I tried to put myself in their place. I never had to drive people from the front. The TCI team would not let me do it. The colleagues understood that I was more effective in strategic planning and partnership development. But on days when all TCI vehicles worked in the south and we needed to transport someone to the Polish border, I offered to help. Of course, the road to Lviv is safe and the trip takes only two or three hours. It is not the same as being at the front near Mykolaiv. But even those "insignificant" trips were emotionally trying. I understood that I was taking those people on a one-way trip. Most of them would not return to Ukraine. My passengers shared their experiences. Each story was disturbing. Sometimes I did not want to believe that what they told me was possible. And there were times when a short and seemingly unexciting story struck me deeply and stayed with me for a long time. I remember somebody telling me of what was going on at the train station in Lviv during the first days of the war. Refugees would drop their suitcases at the platform in a hurry to get on the train bound for Poland fearing there would be no place left. The train was departing, and there were huge piles of suitcases lying on the ground. Such stories make your heart ache; you feel a lump in your throat and tears fill your eyes. And this is only my limited experience. Who can imagine what our drivers encountered when they went to the areas affected by war, danger, and pain?

Anything could happen to a volunteer on the road: from a little mishap and traffic jam to a life-threatening situation. Even if no complications arose during the trip, there was one unchanging factor: passengers greatly affected by the war. When they got to a safe place, they experienced strong emotions, and a volunteer could not remain unaffected—he had to listen to them and comfort them. Sometimes the very look of the refugees was telltale evidence of what they had been through. Once you have seen refugees—their dull, teary eyes, their brokenness caused by the circumstances, the little they have been able to take with them from home and squeeze into small traveling bags or backpacks—you can understand how quickly the anger against the enemy can rise in your heart. And the driver would involuntarily see in this passenger his relative, friend, or neighbor still suffering under the yoke of "the Russian world" in Kherson.

How painful are the stories of the scenes one sees on the road, for example, when an evacuation bus takes a bathroom stop and women are not embarrassed to do their thing right next to men. It is the war that is responsible for this debasement and dehumanization. The driver is doomed to see things like that during each trip, which can cause a nervous breakdown, and emotions can prompt him to yield to a temptation and step on the gas to escape from reality. That was why the protocol prescribed obedience to speed limits.

Realizing possible dangers, a controller contacted a convoy at certain times to confirm its location. During the crisis, it is crucial to double-check the information. Following the protocol, the drivers took turns and ate in the cars (those vacuum-packed hot dogs from Germany). There were almost no stops for sleep. The night stopovers were planned according to curfews because special permissions were needed to travel by night. The drivers slept from six to eight hours.

It was Serhiy Bolotov who helped establish the system of such complicated logistics. He paid a high price for that. After all, besides the volunteer work, he and his colleagues continued to publish the newspaper. They did it even when the occupants in Kherson treacherously appropriated the brand of that paper and began publishing it as a Russian periodical. Serhiy did not abandon his project on which he had been working for years. He and his colleagues printed and distributed the paper in various Ukrainian cities. Besides, Serhiy's family found itself in a difficult situation. His wife had a back problem and she often had to stay in bed. He could not go to her because she was abroad, so he had to call their young daughter constantly and help her with advice as to how to get ready for school, what to put on. Serhiy's endurance was admirable. And this is just one of many such stories one hears during the war.

Evacuating people implied a lot of work. Our vehicles were wearing out fast because of overuse (sometimes as soon as the convoy returned, the vans were gassed, and new drivers immediately took them back to evacuate more people). The vehicles broke down constantly—remember the misadventures with our white Mercedes. We tried to raise funds to repair our "horses" all the time.

But having to repair vans constantly was not our only problem. It was often hard to get gas. Since the very beginning of the war there had been a deficit of gas. Russians destroyed strategic oil refineries. To deal with constant gas shortages, TCI created a special storage facility in the garage. We kept about a ton of fuel: 600–700 liters of diesel and 300–400 liters of benzine. That wise decision reduced the delays on the road to a minimum. Now each driver left Ivano-Frankivsk with a full tank and some canisters of fuel in the trunk, just in case. But the plan was for each driver to try to gas the van at the gas stations as much as possible. Amazingly, every such detail taken into account facilitated better results. In the process, our professionalism was crystallized.

I think that our willingness to broaden the term "volunteer" facilitated our effectiveness. In the period of peace, a volunteer is a person who works for the common good in his free time. War sets other rules. Of course, many people take burdensome responsibilities without receiving any payment. We noticed that it did not work for long. People's emotional involvement during the time of war increases. Volunteers face exhaustion and emptiness more often. Besides, after volunteering, a person has to go back to the job that pays the bills. War reduces his chances to do that. Thus, it is hard for volunteer organizations to carry out long-term projects because there are not enough people to do that. It is wise to note the effectiveness of those establishments that do not try to get by using free labor but develop a structure and institution. TCI wanted to go long term, so we decided to support our volunteers. We would encourage organizations and partners to give us money for administrative expenses as well. We used those finances, not the ones allotted for humanitarian aid, to pay TCI volunteers. Of course, it was not like a salary per se; it was much smaller. But it did help support volunteers and execute humanitarian projects.

This is an example of the flexibility we exercised. We wanted to serve our country for a long time; therefore, we were open to learning from the experience of various organizations. We benefited from the consultations with successful volunteer teams and representatives of various foreign institutions.

Ethan came to Ukraine and did trainings from time to time. Sometimes he brought retired military men who served in different parts of the world, for example, to help evacuate embassy staff or children with special needs from dangerous places. I remember our conversations with two military men during a supper. It was not some special meal—just a regular dinner for refugees that we shared after a day of training. All the participants went to rest in their rooms, but we stayed with the guests in the dining hall.

Ethan's friends shared their life stories. I was touched when they told how they helped rescue a group of civilians in Iran, how they had to hide from patrols and walk fifteen kilometers. The stories were accompanied by the explanation of professional nuances. I realized that the activity of military men is a real science that has some set rules and regulations despite the diversity of the situations people have to deal with. For example, it is impossible to foresee the behavior of a person who poses a threat, but it is possible to calculate the time needed to run away or prepare for defense. It was then that I heard about the twenty-one-foot rule for the first time. The military shared it with me eagerly.

If a trained military man sees a dangerous person with a knife or baseball bat, the distance of less than twenty feet poses a threat. When a danger is twenty-one feet away, a person has enough time to draw a gun and disarm the attacker. This is why quality training includes this principle. It is important to exercise and stay fit in order to avoid letting a threat come closer than twenty-one feet.

That example prompted me not only to deeper reflection, but also to encouraging TCI staff to go through regular trainings. During the war we all had to learn to assess the risks in any situation and avoid letting a danger come closer than twenty-one feet. I also understood that training helped form a team. We needed to establish a working institution while being thousands of miles from home. War and evacuation deprived TCI of many experts. To continue the work, we needed to focus on building the team and partnerships.

Of course, we would not have been able to do all the work we did without partnering with other seminaries. The initiative to establish Refugee Help Fund bore its fruit. First of all, it facilitated unity. Friendship between different seminary workers has existed since the 1990s, and the war promoted closeness. On the fourth day of the Russian invasion, nine seminaries located in Ukraine and other former Soviet countries produced an official statement to condemn the Russian aggression and call Christians to pray. But the educational institutions did not stop at that. Many Ukrainian seminaries united. So, I can't say that TCI has been the only one to help the country. We have always been dependent on the assistance of others.

Most often, our volunteers and the people they evacuated from Kherson would make a one-night stopover in Odesa seminary on their way to the west. One time we did an evacuation with the seminary in Kremenchuk. The believers in Mykolaiv also provided much help: there were cases when people were transported in boats across the Dnieper River from the occupied territory so that our volunteers could take them to a safe place. We made arrangements with taxi drivers to bring people out of Kherson secretly. We used every opportunity to rescue Ukrainians from the destructive hands of the war. Besides, since the beginning of March, our convoy often left Mykolaiv carrying food and medicines for Kherson and returned bringing refugees. Sometimes we had to seat twenty-five people in a cabin designed for nineteen.

TCI helped evacuate people not only from the south of the country (Kherson, Mykolaiv) but also from the Kyiv region. During the terrible events in Irpin, our volunteers were under fire for several days. They took chances to evacuate people from that town. My brother Stas actively partnered with the All-Ukrainian Youth Department of the Baptist Union of Ukraine. Volunteers also made a lot of trips in their own cars. Later our team counted over three hundred people we were able to evacuate during the first three months of our volunteer ministry. There was a week when we brought almost a hundred people out of Kherson. It may not seem like a big number. But only the one who participated in an evacuation can understand how much effort it takes to help even one person get to a relatively safe place. We often quoted a phrase from *Schindler's List* by Thomas Keneally to encourage our volunteers as they were about to set out on their evacuation mission: "If you save one life, you save the world."

We wanted to help our people who faced such a tragic period in their history!

Chapter 8

Humanitarian Aid Projects

THE PASSAGE ABOUT FOUR RIDERS in the Apocalypse of John (book of Revelation) fills us with terror. Even if we do not go into theological reflections on the time and place of the fulfillment of this biblical prophecy, but simply look at what has been going on in Ukraine since February 2022, we can easily detect a devilish march of these riders throughout our land. The role assigned to the blackest one of them is the most abominable—he brings famine. In the ancient times, the very mention of famine made people tremble. Just a short time ago, it was impossible to imagine that the Kherson region, a rich agricultural area, would suffer from this disaster. The war has managed to incite fear of hunger during the very first weeks. All it had to do was to block the stream of goods that people needed to live on coming from other regions to the south.

As horrible as the news was of the ongoing catastrophe, Christians and modern humane civilization could not just sit and watch everything that was happening impassively. Response and involvement were necessary. It was crucial to restore the kingdom of God in all the areas the riders of the Apocalypse had passed through. Hearing of the situation in the south of Ukraine and of a potential shortage of food, we realized that we had to provide humanitarian aid. That was what many organizations and volunteers set out to do, making every effort to get provisions, water, and medicine to Kherson. TCI was among them.

I have already mentioned my friend Hans Hamoen from Holland. His call and the support he showed me during the evacuation were incredibly important. TCI had developed a good relationship with World Partners and was now expecting aid from it. Since the anticipated amount of aid was big, we immediately began to look for a place to store it. We were thinking of having two locations: one in Ivano-Frankivsk and another in the south of Ukraine.

Thanks to Oleh, a Christian businessman, we got an opportunity to store the received aid in the village of Bogorodchany (a suburb of Ivano-Frankivsk). Not only did Oleh give us his warehouses, he also helped unload the cargo. I never cease to admire such Christians. These people are successful entrepreneurs and, at the same time, kind men, sensitive to the needs of others. It is not surprising that Oleh is also a pastor of a small church in Bogorodchany. It was very generous of him to let us use his warehouses for storing humanitarian aid for free.

The first cargo of food items from abroad arrived. Some of them were given to the displaced people in Ivano-Frankivsk. But we did not take our eyes off Kherson. It was best to find a warehouse in Mykolaiv, only a one-hour drive away from occupied Kherson. It was not easy to find a suitable place in a location so close to the front line. The Russian army intended to take the city and shelled it often. We knew of what was going on there well enough: our volunteers rescued many refugees from Mykolaiv. It seemed reasonable to have our buses, bound to evacuate a new group of refugees from that city, bring some cargos to Mykolaiv.

We looked at various options in Mykolaiv, and then I thought about one businessman I knew there. Adam was a successful agrarian who also owned a café and a hotel. Besides, he was a deacon at the Pentecostal church many of whose members had studied at TCI. I can't say that we were friends, but I recalled meeting with Adam a few months before the war. My colleagues and I visited Adam to ask for advice regarding agricultural business, because it was the time when TCI intended to acquire hothouses. The meeting left the impression that Adam was a very generous man. I remember that as we were saying good-bye, he suddenly said, "You know, I would like to bless your students with vegetables!"

It was very unexpected, but there was more to come. Adam took a piece of paper and wrote down an order for his warehouse to give us cabbage and beets.

"This is not right!" a warehouse worker groaned as she looked at the unimpressive piece of paper in our hands. "This is an official document; it should be composed properly!"

My colleagues and I could only smile and look at one another remembering how Henry Ford had always fought with his accountants telling them to just take a paper box and put money in it.

I asked Adam to store the potatoes sent by Hans so that later we could distribute them among the churches. Not only did he let us use his warehouses, he also got very interested in the project. Thus, we had found a place in the south of Ukraine to which humanitarian cargos from World Partners and other friends soon began to flow.

Our food hub in Mykolaiv became an important center to help the Kherson region. It all began with one truck that brought twenty tons of potatoes to Mykolaiv. Then there were twenty tons of flour, two tons of sugar, ten tons of salt, and vegetable oil. During the humanitarian crisis, that kind of help from Hans meant a lot. We received hundreds of tons of cargos. The aid from Holland was also invaluable at the beginning of the spring sowing campaign. World Partners sent potato, tomato, onion, cabbage, and beet (to name a few) seeds to Ukrainian farmers. There were also cargos of grains from IDES partners. With the help of Scholar Leaders and Overseas Council we were able to buy more food. Our partner churches actively donated funds so that there would always be food items in our warehouses.

Now that we had cargos stored in Mykolaiv, we had to find a way to get them to the occupied areas. For the sake of convenience, we made food bags each containing eight-to-ten kinds of vegetables. For example, there was a "borsch bag." It contained all the necessary ingredients for a borsch or soup. All that simplified the process of distributing food items among the population. That was done through the evangelical churches. All we had to do was get a cargo to a local congregation, knowing that the latter would distribute it among the people.

It should be noted that the main help centers in the Kherson region were Protestant churches. I think that after the war both historians and politicians will not mention that. Some may even take credit for numerous humanitarian aid containers and large cargos, but it is an indisputable fact that the evangelical churches were among the first to respond to the needs of people, and no other organizations did as much.

The Evangelical Church of Ukraine has always been quick to respond to the problems. Believers have never remained indifferent to the events happening in the country. Thus, during the Orange Revolution in 2004 and Revolution of Dignity in 2013–2014, the believers were in the forefront. The Russian aggression that began in February 2022 extended a new challenge to Ukrainian Christians. Pastors, youth ministers, businessmen, ordinary church members—all responded to it and started to help their people. When it was still unclear how one should act in the new situation, the church simply began to act, setting an example for secular volunteer movements and organizations. Probably, the main difference between the Ukrainian and Russian churches is that the former ones have always been on the side of the people, while the latter ones have been on the side of the authorities.

Locals also made a great contribution to the delivery of humanitarian aid. By ways known only to themselves, through the fields, they brought food into the very heart of the occupied region. Sometimes they had to go through Russian checkpoints where they had to wait to be interrogated by the occupants and have their cargos inspected. It was easy to fall into disfavor of some Russian soldier and get accused of something. We may never know the names of all such heroes. But the service each of them did to their people is invaluable.

It would be unfair not to mention those who helped TCI significantly at that time.

Serhiy Boiko and Vasyl Zyk are two Christian businessmen who became our "hands and feet," as we put it. They traveled all around the Kherson region and reached areas that we could not. We were good friends even before the war. Serhiy Boiko owned a printing house and a chain of secondhand stores in Kherson. He was a board member for six years. Vasyl Zyk was our student. I do not know a more ardent book lover and collector. He bought every new item that the TCI library acquired as well. He had an agrarian business in the village of Kairy on the left bank of the Dnieper. Before the war, he worked with Americans.

Both Serhiy and Vasyl are known for their generosity. For several years they sponsored South Point youth festivals held by young Christians and supported by TCI. I also remember how they helped finance the Warmth of Love project meant to provide pastors and churches in Central Asia with new heaters.

When Kherson was occupied by Russians, we were considering an option not only to bring humanitarian aid from our warehouse in Mykolaiv but also to transfer money and buy food items in the Kherson region to support local churches. Knowing how responsible Serhiy and Vasyl were, we turned to them for help, and they responded. Through Serhiy we were able to transfer money to Christian congregations. It became especially important in the time when Ukrainian banks could no longer work in the city, and it became impossible to execute any financial operations. Even in that difficult situation, Serhiy would always find a way to help the locals with money, transferring it through his acquaintances. It was an incredibly significant help for the churches, which allowed them to provide the inhabitants of Kherson with food items.

Financial help from TCI supported the agriculture of the Kherson region. The occupants made every effort to ensure that all the agricultural products came only from occupied Crimea. But our businessmen found Ukrainian farmers who refused to collaborate with Russians. It is from them that produce was bought. Vasyl would load trucks with onions, cucumbers, and tomatoes and transport them from the left bank to Kherson. There he would pick up grains at the warehouses and take them to Oleshky. Sometimes the food items had to be carried across the river in boats.

The war revealed another side of its horrible nature. Just think of all the harm that stress did to people's health. This is not to mention those who were physically wounded, traumatized, or mutilated. But the harsh reality was that people were not able to wait to deal with their illnesses and injuries after the war. It is hard for sick people when they have no access to medicines, or if the latter are too expensive. It aggravates the impact of the hardships and leads to catastrophe.

"We have no more thyroid medicine," the medics of Kherson alerted us. "There are no blood pressure drugs, and we cannot help people with heart problems. And insulin has been long gone."

That kind of information raised concerns and showed how tragic the situation was. At the hospitals, doctors more and more often looked helpless as they said, "Sorry, but we have no more medicine for hemodialysis." It was hard to hear that because it made one think of many acquaintances in Kherson who were dependent on various medicines. I would immediately be reminded of my father, who was fighting cancer in Kherson.

What will happen to these people?

Unbearable suffering of hundreds of thousands of the old, the young, the sick is all war's fault. Its treacherous move against the suffering ones is meant to aggravate their pain. Someone has to thwart it and help alleviate the agony. Therefore, the delivery of food was to be accompanied by the provision of medicines.

TCI helped with that as well. We received both medicines and money to buy them from our foreign partners. Sometimes the Red Cross assisted us. We wanted to help those who depended on insulin and the ones who would die without certain medicines. We used our finances to buy insulin and drugs for people with kidney problems. It was the most complicated project that our institute executed.

If it was hard to deliver food to the occupied areas, it was much more dangerous for volunteers to carry medicines. The occupants considered each person bringing medicines to be a potential spy who had access to foreign resources. All that slowed down the distribution of medicines. But the locals helped us with that as well. They managed to create a special secret system. The cargo was delivered in parts. The medicine was not brought to a patient's home, but the latter had to go to an appointed place to get it. It was often a shop or even a drugstore. A patient was to come as a regular customer and pick up his medicine. Such an arrangement did not raise suspicions. It is hard to count how many people were helped that way. I often heard my brother Stas, who coordinated humanitarian projects, note aptly, "Providing help, we think not of the numbers but of the fact that each number represents a concrete human being. Thus we carry out God's mission on Earth."

War destroys all we are used to. It annihilates everything in its way, beginning with a developed infrastructure and ending with inconspicuous things that make one's life comfortable. Catastrophe, destruction, deprivation are a part of its treacherous nature. But man would not accept his doom: his creativity prompts him to look for means of survival. He always finds them and changes the course of history. It is the occupation that showed that incredible human wisdom and practicality that discredited the power of the war and its ugly nature.

While the volunteers brought humanitarian aid to people in small amounts, some businessmen also played an invaluable role. They were able to organize financial transfers for volunteers and charities in the occupied areas. Crisis highlights the role that leaders, including businessmen, play in society. They know how things are done. They are good at negotiating and making connections. They know the key people: politicians, local authorities, bankers. They have all that is necessary for cooperation.

I think of the prewar times. I admit that church leaders were not always able to build mature relationships with prosperous members of their congregations. Our "Josephs of Arimathea" need friendships and pastoral care just like all other believers. But sometimes pastors seem to share only their monetary expectations with businessmen. It is not right to see a rich man only as a financial supporter of a ministry. It is important to realize that businessmen have to be on guard all the time to discern intentions and motives of their competitors and sometimes even enemies. With time, they learn to identify their real friends and recognize manipulations of others. So when they come to church, they can get easily disappointed with immaturity and selfishness of the people and begin to distrust everything Christians do.

Vasyl Zyk invested in TCI's projects because he trusted us.

"You know, Valentyn," he confided in me. "I often refuse to give money to people because I see that it is only my money that they are interested in."

Vasyl always liked to talk with me, so I planned informal meetings with him several times a year. One of them took place shortly before the Russian invasion. And now the war showed even more clearly how strong our friendship was. I admire all the important work that Vasyl Zyk did for TCI while staying in the occupied area.

I hope that after the war churches will become a vital stronghold to serve society with the help of those who do so much now. It is well-known that businessmen have a special reputation among the people. This means that they have a lot of influence. No wonder that at times Christianity missed opportunities because it underestimated the gifts and the calling of businessmen. I understand that it is important, at least, to try to learn to create such an institutional model of the church in which a businessman is perceived as a unique gift and not as a wallet. There is a similar problem regarding politicians in the church.

I really hope that when peace comes—and it will come—we will remember these important discoveries and acquired wisdom and continue to work upholding the unity of gifts. There will be plenty of challenges in society after the war. It is we, Christians, who will have to deal with most of them. So it is important to minister not independently from one another but in partnership. Every day the war shows its harshness and cruelty. Individual efforts of kind and conscientious people cannot accomplish everything. No matter how much you do, there will still be lack of manpower. Sometimes it seems that even if all the volunteers unite, it will not be enough to win the war. Yet when each does his part, be it distributing food packages among the locals or creating an effective humanitarian aid strategy, we will be strong. The sum total of various gifts combined through partnership does the impossible.

Because of the Soviet legacy, our mentality is often corrupted by selfishness. This results in the interaction of partners that looks more like one devouring the other. Instead of implementing the vision together, they get stuck. Potential partners watch each other for a long time in order to understand if there is any profit for them. This is a "win-lose" kind of relationship. The true partnership is when everybody wins, not only those who are smarter and quicker, more capable of taking hold of all the opportunities. If the cooperation keeps to the logic of the kingdom of God and not our earthly understanding, then the results will be more impressive.

Therefore, I will never tire to repeat that TCI does not work alone. We always partner with other organizations. I believe that this approach is more productive. In my time, I had to learn and introduce it into the culture of our institute. I remember discovering the idea of partnership while reading *Well Connected* by Phil Butler. The author presents a comparison between opening a hot dog stand at the street corner and building a huge skyscraper. The expenses of the stand's owner, which serves several hundred clients a day, and the budget of the skyscraper construction are very different. There is no tall building produced by just one company. Such projects usually require teamwork: somebody provides concrete, somebody else the glass and vehicles, yet others the manpower. Unlike a hot dog stand, a skyscraper is meant to remain for decades or even centuries, and it is hard to imagine the number of people who would benefit from it. Similarly, today, as we understand the scope of the humanitarian catastrophe in Ukraine, it is not enough to distribute one load of hot dogs. It is much better to build a "skyscraper" of help that would reach many of those who are in need. And it is impossible to do that without partners.

And, of course, we continue to avoid restricting ourselves to standard approaches. When TCI moved to Ivano-Frankivsk and started to work, we were regarded as unconventional because of our friendship and fellowship with non-Baptist entities. One time we shocked local churches as we helped Pentecostals by sending them a ton of macaroni. It was not done in that area. But we think it is important to remain flexible in our traditions so that we would not miss out on important things. It is not only about interdenominational interaction, but about the culture of fellowship in general. In most cases, an ability to communicate with other denominations and build bridges between the representatives of various communities does not mean compromising one's beliefs. It is rather an ability to be a human being on our small planet Earth. If Christians cannot build bridges between themselves, it will be difficult for them to establish connections with the society.

Before the war, I observed Christians acting in extraordinary situations. When a catastrophe, like the Indian Ocean tsunami of 2004, shakes the world, I notice that Christians are among the first to help the victims. One such Christian mission faced a seemingly fair reproach from their brothers in Jesus: "Why do you help Muslims?"

The wise answer of spiritual leaders was, "We do not help Muslims; we help people."

I would like to ask those Christians: How deeply do you understand the parable about the good Samaritan? After all, its main idea relates to who we see as our neighbor. As a rebuke to the priests, the parable points to a merciful Samaritan, a man not connected with the instructions given to the people of God.

It is interesting that a war makes people of various backgrounds unite for a purpose. And sometimes it brings good by breaking barriers.

As we were doing one of our volunteer projects, I learned about two brothers who served as drivers. It so happened that long before the war they stopped talking to each other and became enemies. The war prompted both to help TCI evacuate people. When they met, they hugged each other for the first time in years. They were able to forgive each other and continue the ministry that was so important to our nation at the time.

Chapter 9

Prophetic Voice

On march 17, ukrainian seminaries together with Moldovan ones held a conference called "Evangelical Voice. Russian-Ukrainian War." Among the speakers were Taras Dyatlik, Roman Soloviy, Oleksandr Geychenko, and Ivan Rusyn. I represented TCI. A month later, sister theologians held a similar event. They presented their perspective on the Russian aggression on behalf of women. It was Maryna Ashikhmina who represented TCI there (her husband was on the front line at the time).

The relevance of the event was obvious: European and American Christians did not seem to understand the catastrophe in Ukraine. They thought economic reasons had prompted our northern neighbor to invade the country: the desire to take hold of coal mines or shale gas deposits or maybe to get back "its historical territories." But only we Ukrainians clearly understood the deeper reasons of the terrible war. Russia started it intentionally because it would not reconcile itself to the fact that Ukraine wanted to choose its own way—to be Ukraine. For years Russia fought to prevent us from getting freedom, and it did not see why it should stop now. We are suffering because of the choice we made. So, the main idea of our conference was to raise our voice, to draw the attention of the civilized world to the situation in which we found ourselves.

We had a big job to do: to explain that the problem of the war had not only the economic but also the worldview dimension. The Christians of the West had to see what was really going on and which repercussions were to be expected later. That was why we raised our voice to show to the world that it was the ideology of the Russians, which had been forming for decades, that prompted them to invade Ukraine. That ideology was called "Russian Order."

How misleading the word "order" is in this phrase! After all, one of its meanings in the Russian language is peace, the absence of war and hostility. Within the first hours of Russia's treacherous invasion, our people personally experienced the evil of the "Russian Order" in all its fullness—it was not peace that Russian tanks and war planes brought us. So, we wanted to elucidate the situation in which the Ukrainians found themselves and present a deeper explanation of the religious and philosophical ideas of the "Russian Order." We felt the necessity to show that its effects were as destructive and dangerous as the threat of Hitler's regime and its Nazi ideology had been in their time. Then the European and American communities were not able to discern the danger in the very beginning, so the demon of evil was set free, destroying millions of people. Thus, now we had to raise our voice and draw attention to the fact that the "denazification" Russia claimed to be doing in Ukraine had only one goal: to deprive us, the Ukrainians, of our culture, language, and national identity.

What is it if not another genocide taking place in the world right now!

Long before the invasion, Russia established the idea that she was the bulwark of Slavdom, which also included Ukrainians and Belorussians. But because of the language and Orthodox faith, Russians have a special status of "the big brother" and a spiritual historical mission. This perspective gives Russia the right to thwart the influence of the West coming through the efforts of liberals and freedom fighters who have only one goal: to destroy the unity of the Slavs. So, when Ukraine chose the European way of development, it was not just her decision: it was a seduction coming from the enemy, a brazen deception. Therefore, it was up to spiritual and Orthodox Russia to save her prodigal sister Ukraine from that immoral snare into which the latter had been caught.

The invasion is the sprouting of seeds that have been sowed in the minds of Russians for a long time. Already in 2014, when Crimea was annexed and the war in the east of Ukraine began, the banner of the

"Russian Order" was raised to justify the actions of Russia. So now, eight years later, the people who have given in to propaganda approve the "special military operation"* raging in Ukraine. Many citizens of Russia perceive horrific cases of genocide of our people as a rightful cause. A terrible thing has come to the surface: according to the "Russian Order" ideology, all the inhuman atrocities and annihilation of Ukrainians by Russian soldiers are not considered to be a crime. It is assumed that Russia has the right to wage any aggression against our people and call it "denazification." One cannot help but see the destruction of Ukraine as a result of the "Russian Order" ideology.

With the help of the "Evangelical Voice. Russian-Ukrainian War" conference, we were able to uncover the misconceptions of the "Russian Order" closely connected to the Russian Orthodox Church, which should have been the first to oppose this idea if she still has anything biblical left in her. But looking at the priests of this church blessing the Russian army and sprinkling the missiles that bring us death with "holy water," one can see that the Lord's commandment "Thou shall not kill" is no longer authoritative to them.

What kind of church would sanction the destruction of people?

Our speakers presented a number of theological arguments proving that the Lord does not support such actions or justify the war one nation wages against another. In particular, somebody pointed to the passage in Revelation that describes the throne of God near which many nations are gathered together. Whose will is then carried out if a church is interested in the existence of the world in which there are only Russians and in which there is no place for other peoples?

We had to dismantle many myths regarding the values the Russian Orthodox Church claims to fight for. Take the family, for example: the number of divorces in Russia is enormous. It is a well-known fact that even President Putin got officially divorced in 2013. What kind of example is it for Russians? Cohabitation is widespread in Russia.

* Russia avoids using the term "war" in reference to its invasion in Ukraine, calling it "a special military operation" instead.

So is immorality: fornication and lewdness are rampant, which is testified by Russian folklore—songs and jokes.

Russian Orthodox leaders are not being honest when they attack the vices of homosexuality in Western civilization while there are many cases of this sin among their priests. The information about it finds its way into mass media from time to time. Such things take place in "spiritual" Russia, which claims to be the protector of traditional values.

What about all the crimes and domestic violence?

What about alcoholism, which has always been a problem in Russia? Thefts, murders, tax evasion, corruption . . . ?

Naturally, our prophetic voice was meant not only for the Russian Orthodox Church but also for the evangelical churches in Russia. Very few Russian evangelicals condemned the fratricidal war, claiming to be nonpolitical. Russian Protestants did not want to admit that their inaction was a part of the policy promoted by the state. Evangelical bishops flirt with Putin's regime just like the leaders of the German church cooperated with Hitler in their time.

The most disturbing thing is that evangelical believers do not realize that there will be no place for them in the future "Russian Order." Even now they are facing a moral dilemma. In time, they will simply be "purged." They will find themselves in the same pitiable situation in which Jehovah's Witnesses find themselves in Russia today.

We Ukrainians reached out to the world community through the "Evangelical Voice. Russian-Ukrainian War" conference. Our voice called it not only to protect itself from the "Russian Order" but also to help us.

However, we have failed to get through to Russian Christians.

Even three months after the beginning of the war, when the atrocities of the Russian soldiers in Bucha and Irpin were made known, Christian leaders of Russia remained silent. Their position was not clear, even though we had been a part of the same accrediting association for a long time (the EAAA). When the seminaries of Ukraine, Moldova, and the Baltic states published an address regarding Russian aggression against Ukraine, that prompted all the EAAA members to discuss their attitude toward the war. Thus, a special general Zoom meeting was scheduled for the beginning of May. The colleagues from Asia, Moldova, Ukraine, and Russia participated in it. At the time of the meeting, I was on the trip to the front.

During the meeting, when the president of the Russian Baptist Union, Peter Mitzkevich, began his speech, my brother Stas and I had just left the area that was heavily shelled and came to a Ukrainian checkpoint. The military checked our car and papers, asked some questions, and allowed us to proceed on our journey. We continued to participate in the Zoom meeting.

"Listen, everything is not so simple," retorted one of the Russian speakers.

Burdened by the situation in our country, I was getting angry with them. It was as if we were living in two different worlds. That is, Russians were living, while we Ukrainians were just trying to survive.

"There is no evidence that there is full-scaled military activity taking place in Ukraine now. There are so many fakes. God will determine who is right. Besides, war or no war, we are building the kingdom of God, aren't we!"

I was about to lose my temper. I had just passed a checkpoint with its lengthy, and standard, procedures. There were literally thousands of cars with real refugees going through it.

What imaginary danger could possibly drive all of them to Ivano-Frankivsk daily?

What other convincing proofs did one need that Russia was waging a full-scale war when I personally took my family and TCI staff from the threat of the coming front?!

I heard nonfake explosions and saw a nonstaged burning of Chornobaivka airport.

I have many people calling me daily from the occupied areas. I know them well enough. They are not lying when they are telling about deadly Grads* set next to their houses that shell Ukrainian cities.

* Grad is a multiple-launch rocket system frequently used by the Russian military.

It was the first time that the sight of the man on the screen angered me. Here he was, sitting in a warm, cozy study with many books behind him, drinking coffee from a porcelain cup, while hundreds of people around me had no clean drinking water. It was even more painful to listen to his words, because we had worked together during the long years of the formation of that very EAAA. My heart was burning within me.

"What kind of double reality is this? What proofs do you still need? Your president has started a fratricidal war. Our civilians perish—it is that simple. How can you not see it? What scale are you using to measure it?"

It was not only I who was provoked by the philosophical elucidations of Russians. I remember Taras Dyatlik's speech. He pointed out that Scripture calls sin a sin.

"The Bible says that Cain killed Abel. It did not just happen. Nor was it 'not so simple' or provoked by Abel. In the story of David's sin, it is said that he was the one who killed Bathsheba's husband. The Bible does not go into long, tiring speculations like you do, saying, 'It is not all so simple, maybe something went wrong, or it's just happened'!"

Roman Soloviy, Ivan Rusyn, and Oleksandr Geychenko joined the conversation. One of the brothers put an emphasis on the prophetic voice of the church in the time of suffering. "If we have a prophetic voice, then it is meant to be raised to call black black, murder a murder, war a war! Why can't you use your discernment? Maybe there is another reason for that—you have started to obey the authorities of the Kremlin more than God?!"

It was harder for the students of our seminaries than for the professors. The former could not react calmly to such a hypocrisy of Russian Christians. It was difficult to believe that church leaders in Russia who taught the Bible did nothing to condemn the actions of the Kremlin. Neither their spiritual experience nor their status could justify that.

"How can we now work with them in one academic world?" the students of our seminaries kept saying.

It was true that Ukrainian believers did not receive support or sympathy from Russian Christians. There was only silence, cowardice, or "it's not so simple" statements. Of course, not all the Russian Protestant ministers felt the same, but their voices were just a drop in the bucket. The fear of repression by Russian authorities made many people remain silent and aloof.

But Scripture shows us that God is on the side of the oppressed. He raises his voice for those who are mistreated. That EAAA video conference was organized to prompt our Russian colleagues to raise their voices. But there turned out to be many differences between Russians and us. They were not able to call sin a sin. The war tore away the masks, and it was now a crime before God to stay neutral in regard to moral issues.

We found ourselves in two different worlds. Although it was hard to accept the separation, it had to be done. For a quarter of a century, the EAAA united evangelical theological educational institutions of the former countries of the Soviet Union. It included fifty-five seminaries. About seven thousand people received education annually. There were also other achievements, but what's the point of listing them now? Besides, we found out that Russian seminaries had already formed their own association. We had no choice but to separate from the EAAA.

Our partnership could have continued as before, but the silence of Russian spiritual leaders regarding the war and genocide in Ukraine initiated by Putin made us choose a different course. During the past eight years, we have come to realize our Russian brothers' commitment to the general idea and support of the "Russian Order." By February of 2022, all the "imperialism" in which the leaders of churches and seminars had been formed became evident.

We have long observed the rules being imposed on the members of the association by the "big brother." In present circumstances, it has become unacceptable. I remember how hard it was to convince Russian leaders that we Ukrainians needed to do our paperwork in

Ukrainian. Some seminaries already taught in Ukrainian. The language of our country was blossoming as never before. We saw similar tendencies in Moldova and Georgia. Yet the reasoning of the EAAA (under the pressure of Russian representatives) remained imperialistic: one language, one culture, one historical space. We tried to raise that question because we saw that the issue of national languages was also important to our Central Asian brothers.

I remember our Western partners trying to help Russian seminaries through the projects that were coordinated by Ukrainian managers, but such projects sometimes met resistance. It was not so easy for Russian seminaries to accept help from Ukrainians. The "big brother" mentality did not allow them to welcome Ukrainian aid. One can detect the imperialistic tendencies even in such minor issues.

It was becoming more and more obvious that the leaders of the association lacked flexibility and avoided innovations. Most of the Ukrainian and Moldovan seminaries already welcomed the diversity of methods and opinions and respected the cultural context of seminaries and churches, which made them more open. But because of the influence of Russian schools, the EAAA professed the imperial approach to mission, which slowed down its work.

Somebody said that the "Russian Order" stifles freedom but Protestantism defends it. This sounds right. It was more convenient for Russians to see all those institutions going in the same direction. Thus, our common work faced a choice: to continue as before or to begin to take into account the context of each member of the alliance. Separation had actually begun a long time ago. Russia's invasion of Ukraine made it final.

Chapter 10

Our Spring Will Come

I COULD NOT SLEEP AGAIN. Besieged with heavy thoughts, I lay awake till morning. The war robbed me of sweet dreams, replacing them with countless anxieties and concerns. I remember the time of peace: troubles and cares were of another kind then. Much was resolved with the help of prayer. The heart felt freer.

Or do the hardships of war make me believe that?

A lonely car passes by outside. Spots of light leak through the opening between the curtains and reflect on the wall and ceiling. I can hear Luba breathing softly next to me. The cat is curled up at the foot of the bed; Sherri, our dog, is sleeping on the floor close by. I am glad that others in the room can enjoy sleep and rest. I raise my head and look at the clock. It is almost six. Sherri begins moving on the floor. I know that as soon as I get out of bed, she will take it as an invitation to go for a walk with her master.

Well, it's time!

The sound of my steps on the staircase was muffled. Sherri trotted on the leash hesitantly. When we just came to Ivano-Frankivsk, she saw the staircase for the first time. In the beginning, she was afraid of it and would not go down the stairs from the third floor. Now she was more or less used to it. After all, she had never lived in an apartment building before. In Kherson we lived in a two-story house. The dog was outside from spring till late autumn—only in winter did she stay inside the house. The familiar course of life changed both for her and for us that year.

We went outside. There were several parks within walking distance of our place. Once I made sure there were no other dogs around, I could let Sherri off the leash. Our little "old lady" (she has been with us for almost ten years) could easily be harmed by big dogs.

Sherri is a mix of Bolognese and Pekinese. She is a very peaceful dog and has a black heart-shaped mark on her white side.

I was breathing in slightly frosty air. Spring is usually late to come to Ivano-Frankivsk. In the Kherson region, the end of March is marked with early blooming of apricot and peach trees. There are still no leaves on them, but the branches with swollen buds are full of delicate flowers—oh, what a harm they suffer from night frosts at times! Later, blooming acacia begins to please the eye and overwhelm with its aroma. There is no other honey plant like it in the entire Ukraine. How costly the honey obtained from it is! Every day spring prompts more and more plants to grow. And how beautiful are chestnut trees in bloom in Kherson!

Sherri ran to a bush and began to sniff it, forcing me to stop. I looked around. In the morning haze, the lights began to come on in the apartment buildings around. Some people were still sleeping. They could be envied. I shivered from the cold, gave a slight tug on the leash, and continued walking. Sherri obediently returned to the path.

In Ivano-Frankivsk, I could only see lonely little blooms of wild cherry and apple trees here and there and realize how much I missed all that Kherson blooming and outburst of early spring. It was the same with my inner life—it longed for spring. My soul was like C. S. Lewis's Narnia yearning under the spells of some witchcraft: ice had chained streams; frost prevented the awakening of nature. I realized that February 24 was frozen inside me and millions of Ukrainians. The change of seasons did not please as before. Maybe we would have been happier had it somehow affected the course of the war, but there seemed to be no end in sight. How could one enjoy spring if he had become a bundle of nerves screaming from unbearable pain. Feeling emotional exhaustion, you began to wonder whether prayers had power to help.

I took Sherri off the leash. She began to run around in circles and then left me alone with my thoughts about prayer. I remembered looking through my mailbox recently and stumbling upon a message that made me smile as it reminded me of the happy events of the past: a year before the war, we had partners from abroad coming to visit TCI. Our guests were very impressed with our good tradition of praying frequently. They were so excited about it that they asked me to share our experience in a special letter, which I did. That was the letter I stumbled upon in my mailbox.

It was sad that now, a year later, the war was ravaging our country. The TCI campus was occupied by the enemy. Sadly, not all of those wonderful people who used to be around were at my side now. We were scattered all around Ukraine and the rest of the world. I thought about the past, and the memories spread like ripples in a pond reminding me of the events referred to in the letter. They all reflected the importance of prayer to which the Institute firmly held and which made it a *place* of prayer. Each Christian school has its traditions. The most important tradition of TCI is prayer. These are the words of Martin Luther that resonate with me, "As a shoe maker makes a shoe, or a tailor makes a coat, so ought a Christian to pray. Prayer is the daily business of a Christian."

Not only do we just think that prayer is important, but it has also become our daily act. It is a special blessing, invisible, but real support of brothers and sisters in Christ.

We have been practicing prayer in various ways. Our hearts got tuned for the entire day during half-hour prayer meetings in the morning when we interceded for TCI departments. We also prayed for our partner organization called Pioneer Bible Translators of Ukraine. There were days when we prayed for our Academic Department or our Administrative Department, for our students and ministry. There was also a yearly prayer marathon. We printed twelve prayer booklets for it that included three main categories for which we interceded: partner churches abroad, missions ministry, and local congregations.

Twice or thrice a year, TCI staff got together for a prayer breakfast to refresh each other both spiritually and physically. Usually, one of the local pastors would preach at the event. Sometimes such a breakfast was organized by missionaries living in Kherson. We had fellowship, prayed in small groups, somebody prepared a devotion, and each received a prayer card to continue the intercession ministry at home.

The memory of those wonderful times at TCI made me want to cry.

I heard a rustling behind me and turned around. The bush shook, and Sherri's mug showed among the branches. The dog apparently wanted to make sure that I was still there. She disappeared again, leaving me to myself.

Suddenly I remembered the words of one pastor, "Doctors say that our organism has three states: active life, sleep, and meditation state." I was not sure of the accuracy of the statement, but I was angry with what the war had done within the last few months. When you face war, there can be only one state because there is no sleep, no meditations, and your active life consists of running away from the horrors of war. Even the pandemic with its endless restrictions could not break us. At that time, we even started a new tradition at TCI—Zoom prayer meetings.

War is a challenge more powerful than COVID-19.

Our last prayer breakfast took place a month before the Russian invasion into Ukraine. One of our staff aptly noted, "How can we pray for new students if we constantly think about the evacuation and expect the war to begin any time?" No, we did not have any guarantees as to what was going to happen. Yet our prayer rose to heaven for the number of TCI students to increase the following year.

We did not expect that the February invasion would become such a punch in the gut. We could not even pray. Most often we just did not feel like it. There was silence. Everyone everywhere was living on autopilot. Only later did I begin to notice that some of our staff found the strength to pray biblical psalms—the ones that gave freedom to curse the enemy, prayers of anger and lament with occasional pleas for God to meet the needs. But overall, silence reigned—Narnia was caught in winter's embrace.

"Sherri, Sherri." I called the dog, as I had seen the shape of another canine snooping around. Although he was on a leash, one could never be too careful. There was a soft rustling of leaves caked during the winter—and the pet was at my side. I rewarded Sherri for obedience with a gentle pat, put her on the leash, and went around the corner of the apartment building. Our daily route had to be changed. We went to another small park.

I must say that the cat and the dog we had brought with us from Kherson turned out to be more than merely an extra responsibility: regardless of weather or my mood, I had to get up and serve the animal, and it became a kind of outlet. The daily ritual somehow facilitated inner restoration. Sometimes I even wondered if it was I who took the dog for a walk or she who took me outside. I also remembered what Pastor Tim Coop from Arizona, who had come to TCI in 1998 to teach a Spiritual Formation course, had told us about his prayer walks. I had not thought much of them then, but in Ivano-Frankivsk, I involuntarily began to practice them when taking the dog out. Those walks often became special times of fellowship with God.

I can't say that it happened every single time. But there were days when the Lord seemed to be waiting for me on one of the benches in the park to listen to my forced prayers, which were more like grumbling, indignation, and murmuring. I think God saw my sadness and discouragement produced by problems and sent comfort in the dark night of my soul. For a long time, it was hard for me to pray. Christian music I listened to could not help. I wanted some kind of stimulus to revive me and make me the way I used to be. In moments like that, the thought of where God was now lay heavy on my heart. I usually turned to heaven with many questions. And kept waiting for the answers.

I remember one of those walks. It took place during Purim celebration, on March 16. It is always a special time for the Jews. They celebrate a miraculous delivery from the hands of Haman when the genocide of the Hebrews was prevented. Their Purim joke, "There are so many Hamans in this world, what a pity that there is just one Purim!" is really clever. The situation the Ukrainians found themselves in was similar to the one described in the book of Esther. That was why the celebration of Purim in those March days somewhat encouraged me. It seemed that God could not but interfere and execute judgment on the "Hamans." There was another historical event that also took place during the celebration of Purim and encouraged me. It happened during the Nuremberg Trials in 1946 when the Nazis were prosecuted for all the horrible things they had done to the Jewish people. It seemed like now it was the time for a new trial at which God would do his work in Ukraine. I remember walking with the dog and praying, "How long, oh Lord?"

Suddenly I realized something: God is not mentioned once in the book of Esther! Yet the story reveals all the things performed by various people who facilitated the victory. Both Mordecai and Esther did something momentous for their nation. It means that God acted inconspicuously through those people. It was like a revelation that made me look closer at the situation today. It may seem that God did not work in Ukraine. But we did see the aid provided by the people from Poland, Great Britain, Holland, Romania, and the USA. That showed that God still intervened in history and brought a victory through humans. The burden lying heavy on my heart was immediately lifted. I realized that we had been used to shifting a portion of our responsibility to God instead of doing our part. I saw a picture on the Internet that illustrated it well. It shows a man asking God, "Lord, why do you allow this?" And God answers, "And why do you allow this?"

It turns out that we are his hands and feet. We are responsible for what is going on. And we can change the script of what's happening under his blessing.

I remember the lightness in my heart as I was returning from that evening walk in March. Somewhere deep inside me there was a hope that decisions and acts of men would help bring about the turning point in the war. This can be illustrated by the finale of the British movie *The Mission*, produced in 1986. It tells about events in South America in the eighteenth century when the Jesuits tried to protect

Guarani Indians from enslavement by the Portuguese. After a cruel slaughter of innocent villagers, a politician says, "We must work in the world. The world is thus." But the cardinal retorts, "No . . . thus have we made the world. Thus have I made it."

The movie ends with the words from 1 John 1:5 displayed on the screen, "The light shines in the darkness and the darkness has not overcome it." Of course, I want to believe that the darkness of the war will not overcome us, smothering us in its deadly embrace. Modern Esthers will arise and be given the authority to do momentous things. Wouldn't that be the answer to the prayer!

"Well, Sherri," I told the old lady, "let's go home!"

The dawn was breaking over the slumbering city. I walked with a dog to meet a new day. I remembered what was on the top of my morning to-do list—Zoom prayer meeting with TCI staff.

Prayer!

I felt that the morning walk refreshed me. Although the previous heaviness remained, I noticed that my reflections helped me realize that prayer was still an important tradition, spiritual discipline, and value at TCI. It had not been lost. We had to go through trials, but my colleagues and I continued to overcome them with the help of prayer.

I was walking, reflecting, and rejoicing at being literally wrapped up in prayer. It was impossible not to notice. When I saw the light in the windows of the apartment that Pastor Yaroslav had given to us, I involuntarily thought that it was the answer to my wife's prayer. I am a visionary and a doer, but my wife, Luba, prays quietly and sees the results. She is a strong woman of prayer, and I respect her gift.

I suddenly thought of another woman of prayer—my mother. She often called me from occupied Kherson and told me about her prayers for those of us who were in Ivano-Frankivsk.

And think of all the prayers lifted by TCI staff! I remembered being told recently of someone calling our workers and asking how everything was. He was told that the staff was in a relatively safe place having a hope of meeting again to pray and worship the Lord together. That feedback could not but encourage and point to our core value, which was prayer!

That was inspiring!

One also cannot but rejoice at the testimonies about the answers to the prayers. "Thank you for the support," the volunteers at the front line told us. "We serve in a dangerous place, but we experience the power of your prayers as never before!"

Of course, now, during the war, two opposite tendencies became evident. Many nonbelievers began to seek spiritual answers, go to church, and pray. On the other hand, believers became atheists. I realized that TCI had the power to stand, thanks to prayer. It would help preserve our staff. We would continue to intercede and support one another. Prayer was our lifeline!

Before entering our apartment building, I turned around. While Sherri was patiently waiting for me to open the door for her, I caught a glimpse of the morning sun waking up nature. I realized that my inner Narnia felt some warmth.

"Even though this spring has not allowed us to enjoy blooming yet," thought I, "it will definitely come. We have prayer. We will have mercy for our people through persistent prayer. There will be spring for all our nation! Come, Sherri!"

Chapter 11

Easter Stories

MODERN WARS HAVE A CAPACITY TO DESTROY objects more efficiently than earlier wars. Just think of the distance factor. What could one accomplish with a short sword? How far could a lance thrown by a soldier fly? Picture the trajectory of an arrow loosed from a bow. Today war can turn the life of civilians living miles away from the front into hell. Daily news confirms the death of many of them. Some were sleeping peacefully in their beds or preparing breakfast in the kitchen; others were taking a walk or maybe waiting for a bus at a quiet bus stop in the shade. Suddenly an unexpected rocket comes and momentarily destroys a civilian object. Its "visit" does not give people a chance to think, assess, protect themselves, hide in a safe place. Some of them die. Some see the death of others and are shocked.

Yes, war shocks people with death.

I was reflecting on why it makes such an impact on people and have discovered that modern life is built so that practically nothing would remind of the reality of death. I am not talking of books, movies, and TV, where death is often popularized since love and death are the topics people usually prefer. But when a man faces death in real life, it has a different effect on him than when he sees it on the screen. Reality immediately throws even the strongest off balance.

The sight of death is always unseemly and repulsive. Therefore, society tries to avoid that which can remind of it. This is why at the market meat is sold in attractive packages. Nothing will remind a buyer of the existence of slaughterhouses where an animal dies, its carcass is cut into pieces and given a marketable appearance. Even a chicken in the shop window is presented without its head so that its form would not remind of death. Hunting with the purpose of consuming the caught prey has become a rare phenomenon. It is a hobby for a small percentage of the population. And it is probably only in the villages, where cattle and poultry are raised, that people know how meat products get to the table.

The tragic events that happen in a person's life and remind him of death also get somewhat veiled nowadays. Neat funeral parlors, lacquered coffins, pretty eulogies during the ceremony, inconspicuous hearses, artificially raised mounds covered with brightly colored wreaths. There is not much that could fill man's heart with terror. At least, this is how it is done in the cities. Maybe in the locations where the industry of funeral services is not well developed, a wider circle of people is involved in the funeral. A man dies, and all know about it. Everyone sees the deceased on his last journey. If we look back into history, we can see the whole city coming to watch Christ being executed in the first century AD. Then death was an ordinary event, yet the shock of a modern man can be easily understood.

Since I have already mentioned Christ, I would like to finish my thought by saying that God's Son triumphed when he rose from the grave. Today his resurrection gives hope to everyone. Even in the places where death is rampant.

"It is so good that we celebrate Easter this coming Sunday," said Olena Andreeva somewhat sadly. "But I don't even know if I live to see it."

Her words brought all our staff into stupor. We could hardly imagine what Olena had to go through in the occupation. The news revealed how Russians turned the daily life of Kherson inhabitants into a nightmare. There was a shortage of food. But it was much harder to hear the one dear to us say something like that. Olena Andreeva was TCI registrar. She was not evacuated because she had to stay and take care of her sick father. According to our good tradition, she joined our daily prayer meetings from time to time. It was also a good opportunity for her to share her concerns. Olena continued, and her words made us admire her stand and, at the same time, allowed us to share in the sadness of our sister.

"I am ready to die and meet God face-to-face!" said Olena, tears in her eyes. "To be honest, the day of Easter is not that important to me—after all, I may not live to see it. What's more important is the fact that Jesus is risen, and this gives me life and hope after death!"

Weariness with earthly suffering and unshakable hope in the Savior—this is what we could hear in the voice of Olena Andreeva.

Hope is truly a powerful thing. Right before Easter, on Saturday, Yuriy Birzov, our student and a pastor in Kherson, returned from captivity. For many of us it was a compelling testimony when he could preach in Reconciliation Church on Easter. The seven days of his captivity convinced him of the effectiveness of hope. That terrible week had been a real trial for him and his family.

On February 24, Yuriy was near Kyiv. On hearing of the beginning of the war, he and his wife decided to return to their home city. On their way, they could see endless convoys of cars of refugees. People were fleeing to the west, while Yuriy was going to the south of Ukraine. When he got to Kherson, he discovered that Z-marked armored cars of Russians had been passing through Kherson in the direction of Mykolaiv for half an hour already.

The next two weeks were hard for Yuriy and his family. They had to find ways to survive. They could not get cash because banks were no longer working. People had to stand in lines to ATM machines to get, at least, a little money. It happened that after waiting for five hours, when there were only a few people left in front of them, the ATM machine would run out of cash. During the day, people were looking for food. The supply of medicines was running out in the city. The sick suffered.

Yuriy wanted to help people in some way. He heard that in the neighboring cities of Mykolaiv and Kropyvnytskyi warehouses were full of medicines. But it was not easy to get them to Kherson. Russians would not open a green corridor for humanitarian aid. When Yuriy overheard that some brave souls brought medicines into the city going through the fields and avoiding main roads, he decided to take a chance. He managed to bring people out of Kherson into Mykolaiv, and he loaded his car with medicines worth about $6,000 from the TCI warehouse in Mykolaiv. When inspecting his phone at the checkpoint, Russians found pictures of Chornobaivka airport taken from the window of his house. Yuriy was arrested.

He spent six days in a cold cell. The military constantly interrogated him, trying to establish his connections with the Ukrainian army. Yuriy was given little food and drink. He was threatened all the time. Russians pressured him, telling him that he would lose his son. They threatened to take away his jacket and boots. It was already agonizing to sleep on a hard wooden cot. Interrogators continuously tried to force him to cooperate with the occupational authorities.

"It was a desperate time," Yuriy said. "I had no way to communicate with my family. Had no clue whether they knew where I was. It was horrible to think what Russians could do to them. The only hope was found in the biblical texts. I found comfort in them, and they helped me in my loneliness."

Yuriy was set free on the seventh day. During his captivity, his wife had been looking for him at all the checkpoints, trying to get him released. As soon as Yuriy returned home, his family left Kherson in haste. There were no guarantees that Russians would leave him alone—after all, they had promised to come for him. The locals often heard of torture: ministers and volunteers were electroshocked by Russians, put under water, or made dehydrated and then given vodka to quench their thirst as a joke.

"It was symbolic to get to a safe place on Easter Day," said Yuriy. "I was so happy to see my brothers and sisters in Christ again!"

The release of Yuriy Birzov is one of the beautiful testimonies. Unfortunately, there are other kinds of testimonies—tragic stories of this monstrous war. Why it happens to people is beyond human understanding. An attempt to explain produces more questions than answers.

One of the tragic stories was the death of Leonid Konko, our graduate. He had been in the army and died in the very beginning of the war. His military base was destroyed by Russian rockets so thoroughly that it was impossible even to find any remnants to do DNA tests.

Nataliya, Leonid's wife, continued to live in their village, close to the front line. Russians were approaching. Village authorities urged her to get evacuated, fearing that she would be betrayed by some collaborators, and Russians would arrest her as a widow of a Ukrainian soldier. Nataliya turned to us for help. We began to work on a plan to get her to Ivano-Frankivsk. In time, we were able to evacuate her and the children with the help of the seminary in Kremenchuk.

Meeting refugees with children is the hardest experience of all. I had never seen kids looking so scared. Two boys—thirteen and seven years old—and a ten-year-old girl got off the bus together with their mother, exhausted as if life had been sucked out of them. They were holding bags in their hands and looking around, afraid to say a word.

We helped Nataliya get settled in Ivano-Frankivsk, which was not easy. I found out that she was still afraid to tell the children that their father was dead. They were sure that he continued to fight at the front. Leonid had been in the army since 2014, so the children were used to their father being away from them.

I remember Leonid well. It was hard to see his family striving to survive now. I took the kids out for ice cream from time to time, wishing to do something nice for them. After all, they needed to see good and joyful aspects of life even during the war of which they had already had enough. I also understood that they had to face reality and learn that their father had perished. Someone had to tell them. Easter Day was drawing near, and I thought it was a good opportunity to let the children know the truth. The holiday itself as well as the realization of the suffering, death, and resurrection of Christ could facilitate an important conversation.

I asked Nataliya's permission to talk to the children about the death of their father. After the worship service we went to a café, and I ordered ice cream for them. When we began to talk, I asked them, "Guys, tell me, what is Easter?"

I was not surprised to hear them tell me what they had been taught at Sunday school. I listened to them carefully. Following the thread of their reflections on the resurrection of Jesus Christ, I said, "You know, kids, God the Father raised his Son on Easter and, thus, has given us a promise to bring each dead man back to life one day."

The children glanced at each other with surprise, then looked intently into my eyes. I saw they were all ears as they tried to understand me. Although it took some effort, I told them, "Children, the celebration of Easter gives you a promise that your dad will be raised from the dead one day . . . and you will be able to see him again."

I am sure that one day God will wipe away every human tear—the last book of the Bible tells us that. This means that we will no longer be tortured by questions why this or that has happened to us on Earth. If we look at the passion of God's Son at the end of his earthly ministry, we may have many questions. But they all disappear after we look at his resurrection. This is why I trust in God who raised Christ from the grave so that each of us would have an undying hope!

The resurrection of Christ helps us in our earthly plight, reveals heaven's perspective on everything that is happening today, and gives us strength to go through all the trials, including those caused by the war.

The war does rob people of joy. It also encroaches on the life of children, depriving them of a carefree nature, putting them through hardships. Realizing the necessity to brighten up the not-so-peaceful daily routine of our youth, TCI organized a picnic for them right after Easter Sunday. When we were still in Kherson, we had such picnics often. It was a part of our culture to meet and have fellowship outside worship services and church events. Wishing to show the advantages of that tradition, we bought meat, sausages, and vegetables for the picnic. We found a good place for rest and recreation where we could play volleyball, run, have fun, and enjoy fellowship.

The Easter picnic was a success. It was wonderful to enjoy an atmosphere of joy and unaffected merriment. That helped us forget the trials of war for a while. Yet it also gave us something to think about. As it turned out, young people never talked to the pastor outside of worship services. Church members told us that during the fifteen to twenty years that they had attended the church, they had never spent free time together. That which was a long-standing tradition and a part of the culture in the south had never been practiced here in the west. I could not understand why it was so.

I began to ask around and found out that churches in Chernivtsi and Ternopil practiced that, while the ones in Ivano-Frankivsk did not. It was a certain challenge for us to make picnics for the youth of the congregation, getting them into the habit of having fellowship outside the church walls.

It just so happened that after Easter, we discovered that difference in traditions in our churches. Of course, a congregation can live without picnics and fellowship outside of worship services for decades. But God's salvation plan relates not only to man's sinful soul but also to his body and every area of his life. There is nothing wrong when a church gets together not only during worship services but also in other times.

Easter brings together the kingdom of heaven and the earthly kingdom under the dominion of Christ. Jesus prayed not to take us out of this world but to preserve us in it. I am sure that there are many acts through which the beauty of people, souls of friends, potential of gifts and talents are revealed that do not necessarily relate to the spiritual sphere, but Christ has promised to preserve us in them. Our life in the flesh reflects God on Earth. His will should be done on Earth as it is in heaven. It is a challenge to us to widen the opportunities for redemption on Earth.

When we enjoy fellowship and share food with our neighbor—God is there with us, and friendships are developed. Ministry has its place and plays its part. But recreation time helps use the potential of building good relationships with one another to the fullest. We cannot ignore the fact that it prompts people to get rooted in God. The old cliché remains true: people come to the church because of God and remain in it because of people. So why not make more reasons for joy and fellowship at the table in order to strengthen the bonds of friendship?

Chapter 12

A Long Way from Home

It's been less than a month since the Russian invasion, but about a quarter of Ukraine's population already had to leave their homes. Just imagine, one in four Ukrainians was forced to look for a safe place to live. This is the biggest migration crisis in Europe since World War II. The Balkan crisis created by the war in Yugoslavia at the end of the twentieth century can be considered close in its impact on Europe. It is impossible to relive all the pain and feel the weight of the oppressive circumstances that have befallen even one Ukrainian family. The war unceremoniously encroached on the familiar life and happy comfort of millions of people.

The anguish tormenting the souls of displaced people thrown away from home as the memories of all the wonderful things they once had flashed in their mind's eye. So many times I relived our early breakfast at home on the morning of February 24, when the war began. Oh, how I miss that familiar comfort of home. It is impossible to explain it in rational terms, but somehow you feel that it is the place where you're safer than anywhere else. Being at home is never the same as being in a foreign land. Anyone who was displaced would give a lot to return home. But everyone realizes that it's impossible now. All that is left is to cherish the precious memories reminding us of home.

Even before the Russian invasion, TCI had an agreement with a church in Ivano-Frankivsk to provide housing to our people in case we had to leave Kherson. We had booked a dormitory for the displaced people ahead of time. I also made arrangements that our people have a separate kitchen and not have to share one with neighbors. I can't say that everything worked out exactly as I wanted—perfect and private—but for our students and youth, that small room on the second floor soon became home. However, some of the resettlers admitted that they did not like it very much at first.

There really wasn't anything unusual about it: three tables, a microwave, a cooking stove, cupboards for dishes, and chairs along the walls on 120 square meters of space—barely enough to accept two dozen unassuming people.

During the first few weeks of our stay in Ivano-Frankivsk, the curfew started quite early—at 8 p.m. But our guys did not dare to go out into the city for a long time. Their whole life was confined to the courtyard between the church building and the dorm. In the evening, they would come to the kitchen in small groups to socialize, drink coffee, and pass time with board games before retiring to their rooms. But the kitchen didn't stay empty. Toward midnight, someone would sneak in there to read a book in silence, draw, or call their extended family members scattered in different parts of Ukraine. The typical nocturnal routine became the theme for a photo exhibition by Tetiana Syniy, my younger sister.

"We were sitting with my friend in the kitchen"—Tetiana was sharing her experience—"who was quietly drawing something. At some point I noticed that she was totally in her zone. I became accustomed to seeing pain in her eyes. But now they were completely peaceful, as if she had managed to find in the nocturnal ambience of this communal kitchen something familiar, homelike, something which remained far away in Kherson. Suddenly, I felt compelled to capture this moment!"

This experience spurred Tetiana to pull her camera out of the bag again. Before the war, she was a promising wedding photographer. She enjoyed capturing the happy moments of people in love—snapshots they would remember for the rest of their lives. It was impossible to overestimate the importance of such events—everyone deserves to relive their happy moments through memorable photos.

The war put an end to those halcyon days, casting pain, fear, and helplessness on the faces of people around Tetiana. The happy world of a wedding photographer was shattered. Happiness was replaced by sorrow. Tetiana stowed the camera away. She thought she would never again be able to capture with her lens all the meaningful and beautiful things we all cherish in life.

"For the first time in a long time," Tetiana recounted, "I took the camera to try and capture my friend in her new subtle comfort zone. This shot was the beginning of a series of photos I took in our kitchen. It seems to me that the ambience there began to dispose the resettlers to socializing, fun, and friendship. They felt at ease at this new place—a forgotten feeling left behind in the kitchens of their abandoned homes."

In mid-May, the first photo exhibition, *The Story of One Kitchen*, was held in the volunteer center. Tetiana's photos allowed visitors to experience the moments in which every regular of the resettler dorm kitchen could rediscover the atmosphere of home comfort.

"Photography is a tool one can use to communicate important things," Tetiana said in her opening remarks. "That's why every photo presented here at the exhibition is a testimony that a migrant is not just a statistical figure. Each of us is a clot of emotions and traumatic experiences. I didn't need to look for impressive stories, I simply captured the moments of life of our large company of migrants from Kherson and numerous friends from Ivano-Frankivsk in the kitchen that has become our home. Friends, we will definitely get through all this pain."

The photo exhibition *The Story of One Kitchen* clearly showed that although the resettled people long for the cozy comfort of home, they do not succumb to despair but rather strive to draw pleasant parallels with their home environment lost because of the war. It is entirely possible that the homesickness will not fade away completely even after a while. Even though a displaced person will always feel vulnerable away from home, no matter what this vulnerability is expressed in, whether lack of comfortable housing or income, the key factor will be the decision to endure and overcome. Therefore, one of the three key vectors of the TCI ministry since the start of the full-scale invasion was support for the displaced people. Part of the humanitarian aid provided by our partners was undoubtedly intended for them. No less important was the effort to help people adapt socially, to settle in their new place, which was not so easy.

The immediate needs are abyssal. Finding a job is the most pressing of all.

The unemployment office in Ivano-Frankivsk could not provide many vacancies for refugees—the war was taking its toll on the economy every day. In addition, there was another unpleasant factor: when hiring, some employers paid attention to the applicant's ability to speak the Ukrainian language and where the person had lived before the war. For most of our migrants from the southern part of Ukraine, Russian had been the first language of communication since birth. Some locals consciously kept their distance from us. Some had the "courage" to drop a scathing reproach along the lines of "The war started because of people like you who do not speak Ukrainian and speak only Russian."

Sometimes migrants were offered wages half as much as the normal wages paid in the city. Some migrants left the country, hoping to find work and start a new life somewhere in Europe.

Unfortunately, one of my acquaintances, unable to leave the country, returned to Kherson, saying, "I'd rather live in the occupied city than face constant reproaches here!"

Those who remained needed substantial support to adapt to the culture of western Ukraine.

It also happened that local traditions created a gulf between the locals and the resettlers. Sometimes this even manifested itself in the churches. TCI tried to build bridges and connect people, but of course this did not always work out. We had to approach every situation with understanding and patience. We tried to do at least something so that the resettled people could recover, rather than collapse under the pressure of an unfamiliar environment.

In difficult life situations, there is always an elusive line beyond which a person gives up. War-affected people, and the displaced in particular, are more exposed to this danger than anyone else. This danger is real, because any recovery and struggle for life is successful only when the individual keeps fighting. This will to fight back, this inner initiative, is the fuel for overcoming any adversity in life. As Scarlett O'Hara would say: "As God is my witness they're not going to lick me. I'm going to live through this and when it's all over, I'll never be hungry again."* Therefore, among other things, we paid attention to the personal initiative and aspiration of the resettled people to organize their life in Ivano-Frankivsk, and not just to depend on benefits.

One important observation can be drawn from the experience of humanitarian missions: in addition to providing humanitarian assistance, one should spend time to help put those you are helping back on their feet. As practice shows, people suffer much less and mobilize more quickly when they start to organize their own lives, look for ways to earn money, and support others. Humanitarian handouts spoil people. That is why it is always important to provide fishing rods along with the fish. The example of Haiti, which survived a devastating earthquake, is illustrative. Haitians left without means to survive soon got used to the humanitarian aid supplied to them from all over the world. In the long run, this led the country to become dependent on humanitarian aid. Similar stories can be seen in other parts of the world.

Over the years I saw time and again just how hardworking Ukrainians are. Of course, there is a difference: migrants from agricultural regions are accustomed to hard farmwork, while those from urban areas are often more entrepreneurial and oriented toward small-business development. Therefore, for some people the problem of employment

* Scarlett O'Hara is the protagonist of Margaret Mitchell's novel *Gone with the Wind*.

is finding what they can do in the urban environment, while others need resources to start a small business in a new place. It was good to see that people did not want to live on welfare; they wanted to earn to support themselves, their families, and their nation.

It was a challenge for TCI to recognize these differences and help people when they contacted us with requests to help them start a business. Some had entrepreneurial experience but had lost their business when they evacuated. Others had yet to try their hand at business. In the first spring of the war, TCI was able to award several grants to start a confectionery business, a recording studio, and a nail salon.

It was so unexpected to find the door to amazing employment opportunities swing open. People have worked their way out of chaos and destruction and into recovery—even if these were small steps and unimpressive results at first. Far more important is the discovery that this approach empowers the displaced people, gives them the confidence they need. The grief of their losses subsides. They have no time to succumb to bouts of self-pity. In addition, many become active volunteers, helping organize the lives of others, supporting the military with the money they earn. Their fire and enthusiasm are contagious.

Even the locals were inspired by such examples of migrants. Alina, the wife of Volodymyr Zapadniuk, a young minister from Ivano-Frankivsk, decided to open a sewing shop. Before that, she had worked in the sewing business for a long time. As the war raged on, there was a need to create jobs for displaced people, so she asked TCI to finance her project. We were happy to support this initiative. Alina's new sewing shop created several jobs. We even had a few workers for Alina—displaced girls from Kherson. After leaving their hometown, they found themselves in a difficult financial situation and lived in constant stress. Employment could be a way out for them. And so it was.

After mastering the sewing trade, the girls were eager to work. We learned that the military had a huge need for underwear. TCI started looking for sponsors willing to assist with this humanitarian project and provide Ukrainian soldiers with underwear free of charge. Alina's shop manufactured and packed individual kits that included a T-shirt, socks, and underwear. TCI in turn put in each kit a copy of the New Testament, a prayer book, and a tourniquet to stop life-threatening bleeding when wounded. Up to eighty sets a week were sent to the front lines through chaplains. One could not help but be happy that people who were tired of the war could now not only distract themselves from their difficulties but also contribute to our nation's victory.

Our desire to support Ukrainians extended not only to the displaced people in Ivano-Frankivsk. We searched for entrepreneurs growing vegetables in the occupied Kherson region. We bought produce from them and sent it to local churches, which distributed it to the needy. This approach solved several problems: it provided food to the local residents and stable income to the farmers, which was a significant boost to them under the occupation.

The war taught us important lessons about the need to fan the flame of entrepreneurial initiative from a small spark in people's hearts. Who knows what difference it can make and what fruit it will bring in the lives of those people, in society, and at the front.

Chapter 13

Education That Forms Heart

In spring and summer, TCI continued to help displaced people, evacuate refugees, and deliver humanitarian aid wherever it was needed. Sometimes those projects were hard for us, people of academia, to do. Carrying out a humanitarian mission, we understood that our primary work was education, and we should not neglect it. New times brought new challenges for TCI. We had to help our country. But we were compelled to perform two tasks: to help those interested in getting education and to support churches by equipping new leaders for ministry.

In the beginning of May, Ukrainian seminaries witnessed the sundown of EAAA. Now we were to work in eastern Europe, fostering education and building relationships with European theological schools amid the ongoing war. It was not easy, especially since we were now deprived of our campus. Our property in Kherson had been occupied by Russian soldiers for several months already. From what we heard, the TCI campus had been plundered, and most of the books destroyed by the occupants.

But we were not going to stop; we planned to continue our work. So, in the end of May we met with representatives of international organizations to thoroughly analyze the current academic, scholar, and volunteer activities of TCI as well as its personnel, material, and technological and administrative potential. Attending the meeting were Scott Cunningham from Scholar Leaders International, Taras Dyatlik from Overseas Council–United World Mission, and Roman Soloviy from Eastern and Central Europe and Central Asia Langham Literature. That was an important landmark for our school that year because we secured support from the partners to continue our educational work. It should be noted that at the moment there were no signs of possible change in the war, and the life of displaced people did not get easier. On the contrary, at times, everything seemed to be getting worse.

During the war, TCI media ministry became more effective. I really liked it that our young and creative staff did such meaningful work. In the modern world, where the winners are those in possession of information, publicity helps promote projects. To say nothing about propaganda: its fruit became evident as we watched how the Russians were continually fooled into silently accepting or actively supporting the war waged against our people. All that just proves that the media department is an important tool.

"Education That Forms Heart" was a slogan composed in our media department in the beginning of the summer of 2022. It was meant to define a new direction our organization was about to take. It is one of TCI's traditions to revise slogans of our institution from time to time. In Kherson we had a banner with the slogan "Studying, Serving, Growing." That motto had reflected our ministry before the war, but now we had a new challenge: our people were going through trials that called for thorough character formation that would help them persevere and overcome hardships.

On the one hand, the war produced atheistic tendencies among the believers. The main argument was that God could not have allowed such evil in Ukraine. On the other hand, there was increasing search for God. We saw that people were interested in basic spiritual questions like "how does one pray?" Theology was now in demand. It was especially true for young people. They were willing to study. TCI workers were to roll up their sleeves and point all those people to the education that formed hearts. The slogan reflected our upcoming task like never before.

In June, we had another event taking place: the representatives of seven Baptist seminaries and the Pastoral Department of the Ukrainian Baptist Union met in Lviv. Presidents of the Ukrainian seminaries are a part of the Educational Department of the Union, and the Pastoral Department is an important body that oversees spiritual formation of pastors. During the meeting, sad statistics were presented: since the beginning of the war, evangelical churches had lost from four hundred to five hundred pastors for various reasons. This number is very disturbing. Each of those ministers had to leave his ministry because of certain circumstances produced by the war. Some moved abroad, others were imprisoned by the enemy, yet others had their church buildings destroyed or their ministry cut short. Thus, the Baptist Union of Ukraine faced the task of training a minimum of five hundred new pastors for Ukrainian congregations. It was necessary to develop a basic course that would help grow ministers who could take the places of those who had left.

Speaking of the importance of training new pastors for Ukraine, we should highlight a foreign support. One of the churches in Cincinnati expressed a desire to support us and other seminaries with prayer. Parkside Church printed five hundred small maps of Ukraine and distributed them to congregations in Indianapolis and Cincinnati to encourage the believers to pray. Each card was a little bigger than a business card and had a number on it from 1 to 500. By accepting a card, a believer took the responsibility to intercede for one specific minister.

They also sent us five hundred cards, and we gave them to potential ministers. I remember that I got number 255. Holding a miniature map of Ukraine, I thought again about my responsibility before my people and understood that somebody was praying for me by name. A reminder that people were interceding for me somewhere in the States gave me confidence and "fueled" me to continue the ministry and bear fruit for my country.

Together with the union of Ivano-Frankivsk Baptist churches, we developed a pastor-training program. Everyone anticipated the rise of a new wave of ministers: pastors, volunteers, youth leaders. The latter category was very important, because there was a great interest in and hunger for spiritual things among the young people. We also noticed that during the first months of the war, when many pastors and Bible teachers were leaving, youth leaders, volunteer center coordinators, and Christian businessmen were becoming more active in the churches. As never before, they were taking the responsibility to spiritually support church members, teach them, and interpret the Bible for them.

The development of the pastor-training program changed as well. It had to be simplified and shortened, and yet it now included additional theological topics. Paradoxically, the war made people very interested in theology. There appeared hunger for knowledge, because some aspects of the invasion of Russian troops were justified as being biblically based. The foundation of the "Russian Order" was connected with "special Russian spirituality" and the Russian Orthodox Church. The Russian Order was allowed to invade and run other territories considered to be Orthodox or historically Russian and even kill those who opposed the coming of the "liberators." From the beginning of the war, in the Ukrainian Orthodox churches belonging to the Moscow Patriarchate, there appeared centers that threatened the safety of our country: Ukrainians were encouraged to collaborate with the occupants, bribed with money, given pro-Russian flyers and weapons—all that was happening in the churches, which manipulated people with the help of theology. The Ukrainians wanted to understand theology so as not to fall victim to deception. So, TCI was going to enrich the pastor-training course with a theological component that would help people comprehend the current situation and resist any manipulation.

Besides the tasks to educate and grow pastors, Ukrainian seminaries faced another challenge: What shall we do when the war is over and society starts returning to the peaceful life? Yes, the war was still going on, but the question about the future was already raised. The importance of the issue was emphasized at the meeting of the Educational Department of the Ukrainian Council of the Churches of Evangelical Christians-Baptists. Several months of the war that shocked the world by the cruelty Russians directed toward the occupied territories made us think of the repercussions it was to have for our people. We realized the necessity to train leaders to work with the victims suffering from posttraumatic stress disorder. Therefore, while aiming at providing our students with the education that would form their hearts, we want to train experts capable of not only healing the wounds inflicted on the Ukrainians by the war but also of forming the hearts of the latter.

Chapter 14

A Space for Fellowship

After several months in Ivano-Frankivsk, we faced the problem of our young people leaving the church. During the first worship services, they were together with adults in the main hall, but as the time went by, they tended to congregate in the balcony. It was noticeable that they wanted more freedom in communicating with their peers, a more modern style of worship, a more relaxed dress code. A traditional congregation could not offer them this. Some of the youth tried other Baptist churches in the city or looked at the Pentecostals. We chose not to stand in the way. The last thing we wanted to do was to lose them, so we let them choose a cozier and more comfortable environment. The Reconciliation Church appeared to offer such a welcoming environment in the city. I chose to stay in the church that had sheltered us in the early days of the war. I wanted to continue to preach and maintain relationships with the people who had welcomed us.

From the moment of our evacuation, TCI faced one pressing challenge: How can we help vulnerable displaced people? What can we do for them, so they don't feel like strangers?

Refugees are almost always traumatized by the move. They are overwhelmed by a host of challenges pelting them at the new place. They often have to work harder and earn less compared to their lives back home. They have to build relationships with people they did not know before. Old social ties remain in the past, but new ones still need to be built up.

We decided to focus on young people, who are the most exposed and vulnerable but also flexible and adaptable socially. We had the idea to have a special space for young people, where they could receive support, so that their connection with each other, with the church, and with society would only grow stronger. The solution was self-evident.

We had a wonderful club culture among church youth in Kherson; they had a space where they could meet for fellowship. Almost every church in the city had its own place where young people gathered. We often saw children going there after school to spend time with friends, play board games, drink coffee, do their homework, socialize, and return home in the evening. We were surprised that this approach was not practiced in Ivano-Frankivsk.

We noticed that the churches in Ivano-Frankivsk had fairly developed church youth ministries, but we could not find ministries that focused on fellowship between Christians and unchurched people, nor were there places where migrants could meet up for informal fellowship.

Our Kherson youth began to share their experience of club ministry with local ministers. We suggested that they try to start something similar here in Ivano-Frankivsk. One of those who supported the idea was Volodymyr Zapadniuk. Soon the team of Kherson resettlers and youth leaders of Ivano-Frankivsk started working on the concept of such a club that could buzz with fellowship and friendship between local youth and migrants. At the same time, this space was to become a place of assistance, where those in need would receive humanitarian aid from volunteers, and those who came to Ivano-Frankivsk would be helped with accommodation in the city. Such a project could become a reality thanks to the joint work of both adults and youth.

As the outline of the future ministry started to take shape, we began to look for a place for the club. One real estate developer, a Greek Catholic believer, heard about our charity idea and volunteered to lease his new premises to us for a year with a rather large discount.

Thus, in early June the youth club Filter was opened in the city. Here is a quote about Filter from an article published in an online edition of *Reporter* at Ivano-Frankivsk information portal. "Khersonians and Frankovians opened a space for displaced people to socialize and find new friends. The new social space Filter opened its doors in early June. It unites people from different parts of Ukraine. Here you can come and work, play games, attend different events and just socialize. It is fresh, spacious and a little noisy. A group of young people are playing board games. The noise clearly does not interfere with the work of a few others staring intently at their laptops in another part of the hall."

The idea of the name came from a coffee filter. This new way of making coffee was becoming more and more popular in Ukraine. This was something city youngsters talked about. It began to attract them to the club, where they could spend time with their peers. In addition, the trendy name of the club also served as a useful metaphor telling new guests that there are things in life that need to be filtered out, like negative information. In the context of war, which every day seeks to saturate the minds of young people with its horrors, filtering information is a very important skill.

Soon Filter became a space where people could work and relax, play board games, and socialize. Life in the club was buzzing with a variety of events: some people would gather to paint together; others would come for a candle-making class; there were music and movie nights, language courses, and more. Everything in it was organized with one goal: to provide support to the migrants. It was a kind of vibrant volunteer center offering all kinds of resources, in various ways.

There is one particular story associated with the Filter Club that is worth sharing. We learned that one of the resettled women, Kateryna, had played violin before the war. As she had to leave her town in a hurry, she did not have time to take her musical instrument with her. But we accidentally learned that among the resettlers from Kharkiv was Luthier Maxym. When he left home, he took neither clothes nor food with him, but he took several violins. One of them was a special instrument made ninety years ago. TCI raised money to buy it from him. On the appointed day, in the easy and relaxed atmosphere of the Filter Club, we gave Kateryna her new violin. This gift was a great surprise for her. Now she has an instrument with which to continue her music lessons.

This snapshot of life is just one example of new opportunities to help resettled people. Even though Filter didn't become the space that could cover every need, we at TCI viewed it as another effective opportunity to serve and support resettlers, especially young people. Although they are typically more flexible and adapt easily to new environments due to their age, they are also more vulnerable. They are like those tender green seedlings that are placed in a greenhouse for a time, with the right light, watering, and feeding supply. The seasons of blooming and bearing fruit are still ahead of them, but now it is more important to reach for the sun and gain strength. As much as we could, we tried to create such favorable conditions for the migrants, allowing them to take root and grow stronger, spreading their branches out in all directions, so that they may be better prepared for the hardships of life.

I also recall with sadness the day my older brother left Ivano-Frankivsk in the first week of our evacuation. Saying good-bye, he and I embraced, and I was pierced by the realization that at that moment neither of us knew if we would see and have a chance to hug each other again. I wanted to burst out in indignation at the war: "You are mean and unprincipled! You have robbed us all of the warmth of love!"

Children don't get enough hugs from their parents. Loved ones are deprived of the possibility to touch each other. Family and friends are separated by distance. The coldness of separation and the distance the size of infinity. This is what life looked like for many Ukrainians who were forced to part with their loved ones and abandon their homes because of the war. So much need and so many opportunities to touch, to help, to make them feel loved.

We tried to fill this void as much as we could.

Chapter 15

Marathon or Sprint

I WAS LUCKY TO TAKE BUSINESS TRIPS TO various countries. Getting acquainted with local cultures, cuisines, and traditions, I always tended to compare them to Ukraine. Let's take milk products as an example: because of constant wars and instability in our country, Ukrainians prefer making cottage cheese out of milk, because it is faster. Yet in Switzerland, one of the most secure countries, local farmers can wait for years for their famous Swiss cheese to mature. It seems to me that this is what makes our nation different from the others. We are quick to take the initiative, but we often get disappointed at the immediate results. That became evident in many volunteer projects during the war. Not every humanitarian organization in Ukraine was able to set up its work in such a way that good and socially beneficial efforts would not tire its own workers. Instead of being a slow-paced marathon, their activities were more like sprinting.

This is typical of many organizations in Ukraine, including evangelical churches. If we look at the congregations in western Europe, their attitude toward ministry and projects is very balanced and well measured. But Ukrainians sometimes think that everything moves too slowly. Ukrainian churches are quick to get involved in projects, sometimes without even creating a stable model of ministry. Very few of them stop to think of what is going to happen next. It has to be done, and that's that! So, the challenge that the war placed before us was accepted with great enthusiasm. For example, there was incredible national unity in the first month of the war. It seemed that the cup of our common efforts would soon overflow, the course of history would change, and the nation would overcome—it just could not be otherwise.

"Just look how we have responded as one man and got involved in solving this problem!"

After a while, enthusiasm fades. Disappointment, like a worm, begins to destroy the root of common efforts. Exhaustion. Burnout. As always, everything is based on the short sprint of emotions.

Let me digress a bit. War does not only break hearts, it also affects physical health. I do not know the statistics, but this is a disturbing fact: the war has caused a wave of diseases. This is not surprising. It is a common fact that the root of all the illnesses is continuing stress. War provides plenty of reasons for stress and, therefore, diseases. Even if someone has not got sick himself, he knows of numerous cases of illness in his family or among his relatives and friends. I personally noticed how many people of my acquaintance were afflicted by various sicknesses during the war. Even our dog Sherri was diagnosed with cancer, which came as a total surprise to me.

So, the war continued despite the expectations of millions of people all around the world and millions of Ukrainians who used all their efforts and resources to help their country and put an end to the war. Finally, sprinting wore people out, while they had a long marathon ahead of them. It became clear that something stronger than emotional strength was required. Steadfastness and stable ministries were needed to help people face challenges.

The human body is wonderfully made: it is able to launch compensation mechanisms at need. For example, if a person has a problem with posture, in time the body is able to adapt to this degenerative change. Of course, this does not solve the whole problem. In time, when the pathology manifests itself, it becomes clear that all this time the body has been inconspicuously trying to help by compensating the best it could. Something similar takes place in man's soul—the absence of results brings disappointment. When a burnout comes, a faint hope appears as a means of compensation. It begins to nourish faith assuring that the situation is going to change for the better soon.

Both people and organizations cling to this optimism. But the anticipated result does not come, and everything remains the same or even becomes worse. This brings a new wave of disillusionment and disappointment. It's not that the faith in victory is not needed—quite the contrary! But we have to acknowledge an uncomfortable reality that differs from our desires. This reminds me of the story of Admiral Jim Stockdale,* who was a prisoner of war in Vietnam for eight long years. When asked who were the first ones to die in captivity, Stockdale responded that the optimists perished first because they expected to be freed by Christmas. But Christmas would come and go, and the anticipated deliverance would not happen. Then those prisoners began to believe optimistically that they would be freed by Easter. Yet they remained prisoners even after Easter. Then there was another Christmas, and so on. That wore people out.

So, what helped Jim Stockdale survive the horrors of imprisonment in Vietnam?

It was a combination of the steady assurance of the anticipated result and acceptance of the harsh reality. This is, of course, a paradox, but this combination is what all the Ukrainians need today. This is why most of the volunteers and humanitarian organizations were worn out several months after the beginning of the war. They were killed by the "optimism," assurance that the course of the war was going to change very soon, by this or that day or following a certain event. Instead of employing the approach of Stockdale, people expected results too soon. There was no long-term strategy to use human resources in such a way that volunteers would have a chance to rest emotionally after working under difficult circumstances. Of course, war is not going to be easy on anyone. Yet we still have options to distribute efforts in such a way that our marathon would last long and lead to victory.

I remember one rabbi saying that every year, during the Passover Seder,** Jews remember the hard times of the Egyptian slavery and great deliverance from Pharaoh's oppression. This is a reminder that

* Jim Stockdale was a prisoner of war from 1965 till 1973 during the war in Vietnam. His example as an officer who showed perseverance during trials helped many captives survive tortures and live till the end of their imprisonment.

** The Seder is family dinner in Jewish families held on the eve of the Passover.

hardships and troubles are a part of human life. They will always be present in human existence. At the same time, God who was with the forefathers in Egypt and used Moses to deliver them will help today as well. He knows how to make a path through the waters of the Red Sea. He has not forgotten the recipe of manna in the desert. Therefore, Jewish wisdom encourages us to hope in the God of Israel and go through trials with him. This approach is completely different from the one that prompts people to believe that life should always be without troubles and luck should accompany them all the time.

I understand that just like any other organization, TCI had to face a sobering reality of war, and we were at times affected by our "optimism"—unjustified and destructive. But we forced ourselves not to get overly attached to expected results. Besides, we revised our approach to volunteer work and added new aspects to make it more effective and stable. We built our institutional structure for long-term work and increased the scope and possibilities of our partnerships. That approach helped our "flywheel" of volunteer work and relief ministry rotate without stopping. Another aspect should be noted: we never hesitated to ask for help, which brought almost miraculous results.

For example, because we had an ongoing need to fix our vehicles, which were constantly used for evacuation, we turned to our partners at IDES asking them to provide necessary tools to do the repairs. Besides, our partners from the Netherlands gave us a small truck to transport humanitarian aid. We were glad that our vehicle fleet was growing, and we had more opportunities to help our people, but we needed technical support from time to time.

The response of IDES seemed a bit alarming at first: "We do not want to help you with repairs."

TCI is no stranger to hardships, so we were ready to accept any answer, but the response of our partners surprised us.

"We want you to evacuate people, not to do repairs. So, we would like to buy you not tools but vans!"

Our jubilation knew no bounds—we got a check for two vans! We were to buy two good modern vans!

"They do not have to be new vans, but they should not be more than five years old, so that you could continue to evacuate people," said IDES representatives.

It was another miracle!

I'm telling all this so that TCI would continue its marathon and not burn out after a short-term sprinting. The list of things we needed to do for our people kept growing. Thus, in July, we and our Dutch partners were able to participate in several projects. They are very heartwarming and worthy of telling.

A school in Rotterdam invited its students to participate in a charitable initiative: each pupil was to pack a small backpack with school supplies and a toy for a child in Ukraine. That became a great help for the displaced people living in Ivano-Frankivsk. The first shipment included a hundred backpacks. Later another container came for two hundred people. It is impossible to describe the eyes of the children as they were receiving the gifts. There was so much happiness and excitement, so much joy. In moments like this, you understand that your efforts are worth it!

There was another charitable initiative that TCI did together with a seminary in Wroclav, Poland, and a Lutheran fund to help volunteers. We knew that people who are involved in ministry had to move around the city a lot daily, and not all of them had enough money to pay for public transportation. So, we decided to help them with that. Together with our partners, we bought about twenty bikes to make it easier for volunteers and displaced people. Later we bought more bikes. All in all, we purchased about fifty bikes, which was a great help for hundreds of refugees. That project was another way to meet the needs of the people.

It was great that we were not burning out—we were helping our fellow citizens.

Chapter 16

Daughter's Wedding, Father's Heartbreak

JULY 2022 IN IVANO-FRANKIVSK TURNED OUT to be very homey and cozy for me. That's how I remember it. Perhaps it had something to do with the wedding of my daughter Sonia. The big day for her and her fiancé, Yaroslav, was scheduled for Friday, July 22.

I'm no different from those parents who don't realize how their children could grow up so quickly. In my case, it happened rather abruptly. When we were still living in Kherson, I noticed that Sonia began to spend more time with Yaroslav, and my son Kirill became friends with Anya. Maybe in your head you realize that these are the signs and bells telling you that your kids have grown, but you do not take them seriously at first. All the more, you do not think that in a couple of years your nest will be empty. Before you know it, your children introduce you to your future in-laws. And then the engagements, the setting of the wedding dates, and the celebration of the union of two hearts follow so soon.

Neither of my children was engaged when the Russians invaded Ukraine. When my family evacuated, Yarik (this is how we call Yaroslav) left with us. Unfortunately, Anya was not allowed to join us by her parents, but she and her sister were able to leave the occupied Kherson at a later time.

A couple of months after our stay in Ivano-Frankivsk, Yarik and Sonia came to us to discuss what was troubling them: "We were determined to have a wedding upon graduation. But now we are noticing more and more how emotionally difficult it is for each of us because of this war. We thought it would be easier for both of us if we didn't put it off, but got married now."

I noticed that other young couples experienced very similar emotions and made similar decisions. I remember that before the war, young people did not have this sort of outlook on marriage. It was enough for them to be friends and date for many years. With the outbreak of the war, it was as if time shrank, pushing them to look at marriage at a different angle. Young men and women everywhere started families. Some explained this phenomenon by the desire to have time to live, and others attributed it to the growing responsibility that arose in the first months of the war. Of course, it was noticeable that under the weight of the difficulties, Ukrainians were rethinking the sphere of responsibility: they donated their last money to the army, they opened their homes for migrants, some went to the front. The proof that our people stepped to a new level of responsibility is the fact that the demand for alcohol decreased during the first months of the war. I assume that there was an increase in responsibility among young people also in the issue of creating a family.

On the other hand, the war took a toll on already existing families. I know that divorce statistics are going through the roof. In each case, it may have seemed as if the marriage collapsed overnight. In reality, the spouses did not want to continue living together because their relationship had long been dead. The war was just a catalyst that pushed them to make this radical decision. How much this contrasted with the decisions of many young people in love who had declared honestly and publicly about their decision to start a family!

So, we got to Sonia's wedding-planning meeting.

We met with Yarik's parents in a café near the town hall in the center of Ivano-Frankivsk to discuss how we could organize and hold this event in the midst of the war. It was still not easy for us migrants, even though we had lived in the new city for a few months, to solve everyday problems, much less to find a place and hold a wedding. In Kherson we knew how to organize a wedding celebration. The financial situation was yet another hurdle. We did not want to incur additional expenses—you do not know what challenges you can expect in the next month. Thus, we decided not to throw a big party because, after all, we had a war in the country and people were dying on the front every day. Yarik's older brother volunteered from the first days of the war and continues to be on the front line.

From Yarik's parents we learned that our grandmothers had known each other since the end of World War II. They and then their children had been family friends for several decades. It was so interesting to learn this unusual fact about our families' past.

The wedding preparations began. Things began to fall into place in an amazing way. I remember I was contacted by representatives of a Presbyterian church in Evanston, Illinois. We were discussing humanitarian projects for Ukrainians affected by the war, when suddenly Carol Weinberg asked: "Valentyn, did anyone ask about your personal needs during the war?"

I had never given it much thought. In most cases, one asks questions about the country, the people, the organization, and it is not customary to inquire about the leader's personal needs. So, I was not able to answer quickly. But Carol's next question was about me personally: "Is there anything we can do to help your family?"

This prompted me to mention that we were trying to put together a small family celebration: getting our daughter married. A few days later, the necessary amount to pay for the wedding expenses arrived in my account.

Soon in the suburbs of Ivano-Frankivsk, Sonia and Yarik found and rented a hall for the wedding reception. It was a small retreat center with a fairly good hall, a kitchen, and a hotel with three rooms. Everything worked for us; moreover, when the owners found out that we were resettlers from the south of Ukraine, they gave us a discount. The place was very picturesque: the outskirts of a small cozy village, Bogorodchany, with a beautiful view of the mountains and forest. Before the war, wedding ceremonies were held here outdoors, in a special white tent. Now a big canopy could be targeted by the enemy, so it had been dismantled.

Finally, the big day had come!

I walked Sonia down the aisle. It was a very exciting moment for me as a father. As we walked down the aisle through the few rows of guests to the wedding venue, I remembered the moments of my daughter's growing up. I thought that not so long ago I held this little girl in my arms, then took her to kindergarten (I remember how she did not like to stay there). . . . First grade! Sonia went to the same school as Kirill (he is two years older than she, so we knew that he would not allow anyone to offend her). I won't forget the teachers' complaints about her falling asleep in class . . . the worship band at church where Sonia played guitar . . . our home evenings in the kitchen when we all played board games together . . . a summer family trip to Europe . . . going to university . . .

And here I am already giving Sonia's hand into the hand of her chosen one!

It is difficult for me to describe the feelings that overwhelmed my heart. The word "brokenness" comes to mind, but not in the negative sense where some grief or misfortune breaks the foundation of a person's heart. It was as if a piece of my heart had been taken out of me. Later, in the middle of my wedding speech, I said: "When we marry, we promise our wives to give them our hearts forever. But now our grown daughters are getting married, and we fathers realize that they are the ones who steal our hearts when they leave their parents' home."

Of course, the reception did not take that long—from four in the afternoon to eight in the evening. The curfew started shortly thereafter, and it was important that everyone was home before it started. The marriage ceremony for Yarik and Sonia was conducted by my younger brother Stas. Even though we have a very large family, it was impossible to invite them all to the celebration. Someone was in the occupied territories, others had left the country, someone had long lived abroad, and it would have been difficult for them to travel from far abroad in this troubling time. But the wedding was celebrated in a wonderful family atmosphere nonetheless!

The family sent their video greetings, and we watched them on the video projector during the party and rejoiced with them. It was funny to see how Sherri (our dog, whom I have already mentioned many times) recognized my father's voice. Sherri is a very active, sometime overly fidgety dog, but suddenly she froze and listened attentively to my father's greetings to the newlyweds. She could tell that the voice was of someone familiar. Sherri's role in Sonia's life and wedding deserves a short story.

The bonds of Sonia and Sherri's friendship reach back a decade. I remember a time when my teenage daughter dreamed about a dog. My wife and I pushed back on her pleas for a long time, but finally we gave in. We started looking for a good option among our acquaintances. It just so happened that Sonia's friend Kateryna Lubyana's dog gave birth to a few puppies, and she was giving out puppies to her friends. That's how our family got a little pet (a cross of a Bolognese and a Pekinese). There were several black spots on the white body of the puppy. One spot was in the shape of a heart, which in every way complemented the good nature of Sonia's new friend. My daughter gave the dog a very affectionate name—Sherri—and she became a member of our family. She even accompanied us on our small trips; for example, when we went to my wife Luba's sister in Nova Kakhovka, Sherri often accompanied Sonia. How happy Sherri was when I returned from business trips at night! She barked, jumped, rejoiced, sniffed the travel bags!

When we were forced to leave Kherson, we had to take the dog and the cat with us. Here in Ivano-Frankivsk Sherri has become an extra source of joy for us. It is nice to see her greeting me every time I come home from work in the evening, expressing her happiness!

During the wedding, one of my daughter's long-held wishes came true. Sonia dreamed that her little furry friend Sherri would bring the wedding rings down the aisle. So, we tied a box with wedding rings to the harness that was put on the dog ahead of time. But everything did not go as expected: Sherri was in such a hurry to bring her master the box with the rings that she dropped it on the way, and we had to pass this important attribute of the celebration through the bridesmaid. The incident was very amusing for everyone, both the guests and the newlyweds!

It was a little unusual to see happiness and joy on the faces of people close to us. One of the reasons that was so rare was that most of the guests at the wedding were resettlers from southern Ukraine. The very fact of joy about the creation of a new family speaks of an important and wonderful hope and future. Sharing this joy with other resettlers, one involuntarily recalls the words of Mother Teresa, who answered the question "how can one make a difference in the world?" by saying, "Go home and love your family." On the other hand, if you look closely at the tyrants starting brutal wars—from Hitler to Putin—they are lonely and miserable people who sometimes have nowhere to return to in the evening but a luxurious and cold palace that protects them from their enemies. They are surrounded by opportunists and self-serving people, constrained by low interests, corruption, and embezzlement. Tyrants have no personal happiness and do not want to allow anyone on Earth to have it. This is the nature of a flawed person who has reached unlimited power.

That's how our wedding celebration went. Kirill and his fiancée, Anya, participated in the preparations for Sonia's wedding. Kirill did not mind getting married that summer either, but because Anya's parents were still in the occupied city, they decided to wait until Kherson was liberated. They wanted to see Anya's parents at their wedding.

I remember another couple from Kherson who traveled with us on the first day of the war in a white van—the very one we managed to buy early in the morning at the car market. They had a wedding planned for February 25, 2022. They had already rented a place for the celebration and bought the necessary products, and the bride had chosen a wedding dress and invited guests. The newlyweds rented an apartment, where they planned to start their family life after the wedding.

The day before the cherished date, the war broke out. The groceries disappeared. The flowers wilted. The dress was left hanging in the closet. Instead of a wedding trip, the bride and groom were forced to evacuate in a van, which stalled from time to time on the way. It wasn't until a few months later that they were able to get married away from their hometown. It was a modest celebration, in the church with a yellow facade on Hordynskoho St. Only resettlers and the pastor of the church, Serhiy Mykhailovych, were present at the celebration. After the wedding, young people in the dorm converted a storeroom into a bedroom for them, into which the husband and wife moved for a few weeks before they could rent a room in the city.

I remember another wedding, where the groom was drafted to the front. Before he left, he decided to get married in a church to the love of his life. He said that it was important for him to know that his wife was waiting for him at home, that he had a clear understanding of what he was going to fight for.

I've already mentioned that the war not only spurred young couples to tie the knot but also destroyed many marriages. I can't forget a phone conversation I had with one of the volunteers. He was helping to bring many families, children, and women out of the regions under shelling. He sent his wife and children to Romania to protect them from the war.

"Valentyn!" he cried into the receiver. I remembered this conversation in detail. "It looks like my wife is breaking up with me. In the last call she said: 'I probably won't be coming back to you. If you can leave Ukraine, I won't mind, but I won't come back.'"

"But wait." I tried to gather my thoughts. "If I'm not mistaken, you've been married for more than ten years. What could have happened?"

"I don't know what happened to her."

There was a long pause. I could feel how hard it was for him—his world had turned upside down overnight. Suddenly I remembered: "What about your children?" I asked.

He sighed. "She said it was my problem."

Pictures of a possible scenario for this family, which looked normal just recently, flashed before my eyes.

I remembered another case when a wife, risking everything, returned from a safe place in Europe to warring Ukraine to her husband—"I can't live without you. It's hard for me without our family!" I really wish that there were more of these because a strong family bond between spouses always projects the image of a brighter future and stability, and that is what our nation needs, especially now. When you think about how such decisions affect the lives of the next generation, you grow even more worried. This topic is close to me, because one of my hobbies has helped me to understand this better.

The events of the last few months had sometimes left me so empty in the evenings that I had no interest in anything. After a hard day's work, I didn't feel like doing anything. No desire for books. No desire to watch movies. I did not know what to do to distract myself from routine and oppressive thoughts. I don't know how it happened, but I remembered my longtime hobby: researching my ancestry and making a family tree of my family. This was my third attempt. I remember that in 2003 I went through the archives looking for information about my ancestors. In 2009 I tried to compile something in a special program on the computer. Then I put everything aside for a long time. Now, during the war, I was drawn to it with renewed vigor.

I can't fully explain why this suddenly became important. Somehow, I became interested in the lives of my paternal and maternal grandfathers and discovered that the times in which they lived had similarities with ours. The facts of their biographies, the fate of their families, shocked me. I learned that my father's father and his three brothers fought in the battles of World War II. Two of them were killed at the very beginning of the war. One was wounded near Leningrad and came back paralyzed. My grandfather was lucky to come back from the front alive. The family of my dad's mom were considered kulaks* by Communist authorities and stripped of all their

* Kulaks were farmers who owned some land and occasionally used hired labor. During Communist collectivization, government officials seized farms and killed many kulaks, deported others to labor camps, and drove many others to migrate to the cities following the loss of their property to the collectives.

belongings; many died of hunger. Studying the genealogy on my mother's side, I found out that my grandmother's relative and she herself were in Jewish labor camps. My mother's father's relatives also survived the dekulakization. They were exiled to Russia.

Browsing through biographical facts of my ancestors inevitably led me to find parallels with the events that my extended family has experienced over the past decade. By "extended family" I mean the family of my grandfather Pavlo A. Syniy, who was born in 1919. Usually, a couple of times a year our extended families would get together. Often it was on my grandfather's birthday or in connection with some other events. But over the last decade, our family members started leaving Kherson. Since the beginning of the hybrid war in 2014, when the annexation of Crimea took place and the conquest of Donbas by the Russians began, some of my relatives left Kherson for good. My cousins left for Germany. Another cousin went to Poland; some relatives moved to the USA. A few others settled in Croatia and Bosnia. And now, when a new phase of the war broke out in February, more members of our large family had to leave their hometown. When my family and my brother Stas's family, as well as my younger sister, became internally displaced, we evacuated to Ivano-Frankivsk. There were almost no relatives left in Kherson—only my parents. In a short time, we were scattered all over the world. So far, there is little hope that we will get back together again for someone's birthday or holiday. And of course, I increasingly notice parallels between today's events and what happened to the past generations of my family: wars, famines, epidemics, or the search for a better life scattered my relatives all over the earth.

Realizing this, I do not want to lose my roots, or at least I want to collect the memory of my family. That's why I decided to finish compiling my family tree. I was even more pleased when we unexpectedly discovered during the preparation for my daughter's wedding that Yarik's forefathers had been close friends with my ancestors. I think it is important to know and understand that not only events and similarities in life scenarios can resonate through generations but also acquaintances and friendships that show how closely everything is interconnected. This is very much in line with the words of the English poet John Donne, that "no man is an island" but rather part of "the continent, a part of the main." I realize that who I am is in part defined by my roots. As I look around at this time, I pray and wish blessings to my lineage. And even if I feel that when my daughter created her family she took a part of my heart out of me and took it with her, I realize that it is not a terrible thing—it is a bittersweet heartache—but the departure of a brother, with whom I lived fifteen years in the same home and could not say good-bye to, is a wound that leaves deep scars.

Chapter 17

Cross-Pollination

First, we resettlers did not pay much attention to the differences between the south and west of Ukraine. They became clearer for me as I talked and mixed with other Ukrainians who, like us, came to Ivano-Frankivsk from other regions of the country. I think the turning point was the summer camp for pastors, where I was called to be a speaker. I was asked to address the change churches in Ukraine were going through during the war. A particularly relevant topic was the theology of hospitality. Because it is one thing for a church to be able to host guests for a day or two and quite another to continue showing hospitality to displaced people for six months, I was also asked to speak on leadership in times of change.

I agreed to participate. I imagined that a retreat in Ivano-Frankivsk would look just like all the similar events for pastors or men that TCI held annually in Kherson. I was excited to be able to share a wonderful time of fellowship with pastors in a picturesque location with a rich program awaiting us all.

Several local pastors advised me to rent a room in a hotel near the campground. I decided to follow this advice, so my wife and I found a small cozy hotel with a view of Mount Hoverla.

I remember that sunny day on July 25, when we were looking for the venue where the event would be held. The network coverage in the mountains was sketchy, so we couldn't reach the organizers for quite a while. We managed to get to Vorokhta, where the camp was located. On its territory were three wooden houses, a soccer field, beautiful green lawns, the loud gurgling of a mounting river, and all of this against the backdrop of Mount Hoverla. This place is famous for sports and hiking trails—a paradise for those who love mountaineering and winter sports. The nature of the Carpathians amazes at every step!

I met with the organizers of the event. I really wanted to know what the program and schedule would be like. For TCI, organizing camps and conferences was a standard operation. When similar events were held in Kherson, we usually took preparation very seriously. A program coordinator was appointed in advance, and a working group worked for a year. They met twice a month; worked out logistical details, advertising, program, leisure and sports activities; planned the budget; discussed potential speaker candidates and topics to be covered. So, I was a little nervous as a guest speaker. At TCI we usually planned six to nine important topics for three days, and then participants could choose to attend ten to twelve additional workshops. But I realized that I was not in Kherson. I had asked the hosts similar questions three days before the event, but they just assured me not to worry—"everything will be fine!"

The camp schedule looked very flexible. That was a pleasant surprise. On the day of arrival participants could arrive at camp anytime from morning until dinner. The entire program was planned for the evening. Therefore, the participants were given complete freedom—in the sense that everyone could keep themselves busy: socializing, hiking, playing sports, or just relaxing. As a keynote speaker, I was given forty minutes for my lecture in the evenings after dinner.

It was time for dinner. It was the beginning of our exposure to the Carpathian cuisine. I didn't pay much attention to how it might differ from the food I was used to. It was here at the camp that I tasted the mushroom soup for the first time. It was served as a first course in large metal cups, which was an unusual thing in itself. I appreciated that the soup was very rich and tasty.

I also learned that not every mushroom is good for the mushroom soup. As I was told, its important ingredient is the white mushroom (porcini). The Carpathians are a mushroom region, but only the white mushroom is really valued here. All other mushrooms are not considered worth any attention by the locals. I can relate to this by drawing a parallel with watermelons. Our region in Ukraine is considered the land of watermelons, vegetables, bread, and fish. Buying a watermelon weighing less than ten kilos almost seems something shameful for me. But here, just before coming to the camp, I saw people buying watermelon by quarters.

The next gastronomic delight and discovery for me was *bograch*. It's a delicious Hungarian dish. It's kind of like goulash. It includes several kinds of meat, including smoked meat. Also, I remember one day for breakfast we were served corn porridge cooked with cream or sour cream. It is called *banush* or *banosh*. It is served with sheep cheese and cracklings. I should note that such a dish is not typical for our places, although corn grows in abundance there. I met such a dish in Moldovan homes in the south of the country. It is called *mamaliga*. Curiously, I saw a difference in drinks as well. In this part of Ukraine people drink *uzvar*—a drink cooked from dried fruits. We usually make compote from fresh fruit.

The second day of the camp with its flexible schedule brought me new experiences. Immediately after breakfast and a small prayer meeting there was free time until dinner, which the participants were invited to fill themselves. I heard that some of the ministers had decided to go to Mount Shpytsi. Luba and I were called by the young ministers to Mount Hoverla. We agreed. We realized that we needed to fill the time until evening, so we decided to keep them company.

When we set off, I had no idea that the ascent would take us three hours and that about the same amount of time would be necessary for the descent. I really liked that on the first stage of the ascent to the so-called Little Hoverla an increasingly picturesque view of the surrounding area opened up every hundred meters. The sky overhanging us was getting closer. We admired the nature and chatted at ease. However, the last five hundred meters, which we had to cover to get to the top, were very difficult.

I am new to mountainous terrain, and Hoverla is the highest peak in Ukraine (2,061 meters). Not the best option to get "baptized with fire" into mountain tourism. I personally like water expanses more. Can a trip to the mountains be compared to a sailboat ride? The faces of the locals who invited Luba and myself to ascend to Hoverla radiated with genuine pleasure. They kept telling us all about this region with delight and pride. I think I could also praise our steppe and seaside expanses of the Kherson region for a long time. I'm sure it's all a matter of personal preferences: one likes dogs, another likes cats. Sometimes we easily perceive what another person likes, and sometimes we hardly share his views. And, of course, we are full of expectations that someone will accept our point of view. That's just the way we are!

Already after the descent, I thought: Why did I have to climb up that mountain in the first place? I was not prepared for such a long walk. No one had told me how much effort it would take. On the other hand, I have absolutely no regrets that I made the ascent. I have the most pleasant memories from our joint hike and fellowship with new acquaintances. Even so, I wasn't sure if I would ever want to climb up there again.

One positive highlight of the Hoverla hike for me was the ability to listen to other people's feedback. I remember the phrase of Halyna, the wife of one of the local pastors and our guide to the summit. She said during a short break: "I had never been familiar with Ukrainians from the south or east before. I always thought that all of us across Ukraine were very similar. The war forced us to get to know each other better. Now I see how different we are from each other, but that's the big advantage."

I looked around at those who were with us at that moment. I saw pastors from Ivano-Frankivsk and the south, but also from Donetsk and Luhansk. Together we continued to talk about our differences. Someone concluded that this was even a good thing, especially when you imagine how much it could serve the church. We recognized that our cultures and traditions, though slightly different, do not in the least keep us from being Ukrainians.

This conversation continued throughout our time at the retreat. In the evenings, when we gathered around the campfire, the ministers were eager to talk about the peculiarities of the region from which they had been forced to evacuate. I think this was also partially prompted by the topics of my messages. Each evening, I spoke in the dining hall for an hour about God's view of hospitality. People listened carefully and asked questions. I could see their genuine and keen interest in the topic in the dialogues we had. The war forced us to move, brought us together here, and united us in a unique way. The feedback I heard after my lectures indicated that even though I was someone who came from a different culture, with different traditions, there were no barriers between us that could prevent me from teaching and edifying ministers.

I remember a pastor from Melitopol who came to visit us. We decided to have lunch together with several TCI teachers. Over tea, the pastor told us about the difficulties his church was facing. The Russians had taken away the building in which they worshiped. Then our conversation gravitated toward differences between regions of Ukraine. It was something particularly important for our guest. He had been a church pastor for over thirty years, and perhaps more than anyone else had been attentive to the cultural differences in Ukraine.

"Here in western Ukraine, pastors tend to lean toward a spontaneous style of church services," he suggested. "Quite often the preacher is invited to take part in the service right before the service. For us it is more typical to plan sermon topics several months or at least several weeks in advance."

I couldn't agree with him more. I have noticed, too, that it seemed strange for local preachers to develop sermon plans four to eight services in advance. The pastor also noted that churches in Ukraine have different views on systematic theological education. Some churches have leaders who are committed to training, while others do not see theological education as valuable.

It is hard to say whether geographical location plays a role in this, but I have heard of this problem myself. The one thing I fully agreed with my interlocutor about was the different understanding of partnership. I have to say that we at TCI, and the ministers in Kherson in general, have always worked on developing partnerships. We often did joint projects in Kherson, and it was important for us to serve the community and show the unity of believers. It was about such broad topics as youth, creativity, education, church, or community. Here in western Ukraine, this difference became very noticeable in a short time. Many people outside our bubble have noted that we were not held back by denominational boundaries. As a result, we worked with Greek Catholics on some projects, and a Pentecostal pastor helped us with the acceptance of humanitarian goods.

Since the beginning of the war, Ivano-Frankivsk has become our home. I will never tire of expressing my gratitude to everyone who opened their homes and let in brothers and sisters, Ukrainians fleeing the horrors of war. Each of us experienced the hospitality of the locals firsthand. I would be curious to know what observations an Ivano-Frankivsk resident would make when coming to Kherson. I am sure that, having taken a fresh look at our southern living, our life and culture, he would have something to say. Besides, there are always local experts who can lift the veil of history, just as I was lucky to have those who revealed to me the history of Ivano-Frankivsk.

We should by no means oppose the difference of cultures of the south and west of Ukraine, which has historically developed. It is more correct to consider this topic from the position of mutual enrichment. The forced evacuation and resettlement of Ukrainians from one part of the country to another prompted familiarity with the differences not only within the church community but also within broader culture in general. It was a kind of cross-pollination that occurs between plants of the same species when pollen from one flower falls on the flower of another plant.

The peculiarity that is clearly visible in Ivano-Frankivsk is the patriarchal and, to some extent, conservative way of life. People here follow church traditions more strictly. Respect for elders, including respect for authority, is stronger than in the south. Sometimes it seems that the vast steppes of the Kherson region could not but give birth to the free Cossack spirit, freedom-loving temperament, desire for change and openness in many things. For their part, the residents of the Carpathians tend to stick to their traditions.

Back in the Soviet days the Ukrainian KyivNaukFilm studio released a series of cartoons with funny and clever Cossacks. Each new episode showed new Cossack adventures: they would go to get salt, play soccer, rescue brides, or help musketeers, and much more. If we go back to the events of 2022 with TCI and look at what has been happening since the beginning of February, we can say that our resettlement in Ivano-Frankivsk can be called the series *How the Cossacks Went to Visit the Hutsuls.**

What surprised us Cossacks here were the holidays! The west of Ukraine has this most important part of the national culture. Everything from the scale of festivities, to the amounts of food, to the songs, to the wearing of *vyshyvanki* (national embroidered shirts and dresses) says that here they know how to cherish traditions, remember them, and pass them on from generation to generation. As soon as we discovered that *vyshyvanki* is a rich addition to our Ukrainian national code, we immediately adopted it. It is so affordable here that Ukrainians are always in new embroidered clothes for every holiday.

It is good to see that the west of Ukraine has carefully preserved its culture, language, and identity, but one negative aspect is its closedness. This is especially true of the church. Communities are often closed from society. After all, when new people appear among believers, it is important for everyone to be flexible and adjust to the new members of the community. The opposite happens: the newcomers need to become "us," which builds up extra obstacles. Even today, when thousands of resettlers have joined the ranks of local congregations, some pastors have to make up rules to protect their churches so that they remain pure. New people, as members and

* Hutsuls are a subethnic group of Ukrainians living in western Ukraine.

bearers of a different subculture, certainly think and act differently. It shouldn't be perceived as a threat to local traditions. It is not necessary to build defense mechanisms, for they can become unnecessary hurdles for newcomers. I often notice that the church is one institution that reacts very painfully to changes or critique of its traditions. I am sure that this is one area where our Cossack genes, which help us adjust to change easier, could be a good addition to the Hutsuls.

"Uniformity is the main enemy of unity." I do not know who the author of this adage was, but I have often heard it from Serhiy Sannikov. It seems to me that unity, which can be achieved, will not be built on differences. Misunderstanding of differences leads to discord. But if we accept carriers of another culture and stimulate mutual influence, it will always only enrich both parties. It will become the process of cross-pollination, after which the fruit will set and harvest will definitely follow in due time!

Chapter 18

Theology After Bucha

"WHEN A MISSILE HITS YOUR HOME, your theology will change immediately."

I read this comment on the Internet, under a photo that showed the devastating outcomes of the Russian shelling of the living quarters of a home in a peaceful Ukrainian city. One can, of course, argue with the person who wrote it, because main theological beliefs remain unchanged. But it is necessary to revise the context in which we find ourselves from time to time to see what is relevant and what is not. The war between Russia and Ukraine is an example of that.

"Why has God allowed this monstrous war?"

"Why didn't he stop all those horrible things that Russians did to civilians in Bucha from happening?"

"Why doesn't God judge all this inhuman evil right away, but it continues to multiply and bring only troubles to our country?"

Why? Why? Why?

So far, the people in Ukraine have not received clear answers to their *whys*.

There are only questions, questions, questions.

Over a hundred years ago, the renowned sociologist Max Weber studied religious communities and their influence on society. Reflecting on Christian ethics, particularly those expressed in the Sermon on the Mount, Weber emphasized the absolute and uncompromising nature of its demands. He argued that the teachings of Christ did not permit selective or convenient adherence—they required total commitment. In Weber's words, one cannot simply choose to embrace or abandon these teachings at will; they demand full obedience and continuous dedication.

Weber made this poignant observation long before the devastating world wars of the twentieth century profoundly shook European civilization. It would be deeply insightful to hear Weber's perspective on Christians navigating the turmoil of those tragic decades. Sadly, it seems likely that many believers, confronted by unprecedented moral and social upheaval, ultimately abandoned the challenging path of complete fidelity to Christ's teachings.

With deepest regrets, I must admit that the war dealt a heavy blow to the faith and convictions of Christians in our country. I meet such believers. Some of them look as if they had the ground cut out from under their feet. People leave churches. They stop believing in God. It looks like their knowledge of the Bible and of God does not help them understand what is going on. There is confusion in their hearts. The discrepancies between reality and the Sermon on the Mount keep growing.

How can we love those who have come to kill us?

Should we still be willing to do good unto those who hate us?

Why do I find it hard to pray for those who hurt us and drive us out of our homes?

Do we turn the left cheek to the one who hits us on the right one?

In total darkness, even a small light brings comfort. During the wars of the twentieth century, those who tried to explain current events with the truths from the Bible would "blaze up" like flashes of hope. C. S. Lewis is an example of such a light. While still an atheist, he fought in World War I. Later, he came to faith. How beneficial his impact was on the nation when the war with Germany broke out! His radio talks about faith became a source of hope.

Christianity in Ukraine finds itself in a similar situation today. Someone has to revise theology for people. To ask the right questions. To "light up" the answers with the biblical truths. With this purpose, an international conference called "Theology After Bucha" was held in Kyiv in August. Our institute took part in it.

The name of Bucha, once a pretty little town near Kyiv, was included in the title intentionally. Almost in the very beginning of the full-scale invasion, it was attacked by the Russian army. The houses of many people were destroyed. But the horrifying picture was revealed to the world later, when Bucha was liberated from the occupants on March 31, 2022. There were corpses of civilians lying in the streets of the town. Only a few of those people were hit by the pieces of shells; most of them were shot with guns. It was terrible to see that many of them had their hands tied behind their backs. Russian Ministry of Defense denied the involvement of their soldiers in what had happened and called it disinformation.

Later, several independent investigations showed that those civilians had been shot during the Russian occupation. It is proved by cell-phone videos and data from closed-circuit TVs and military drones, which were recording everything that was happening in Bucha. Besides, mass graves of civilians were found as well as the evidence of marauding, rape, torture, and murder. The Ukrainians who lived through the occupation told about the cruelty with which Russian soldiers treated the locals.

The sad story of Bucha stirred the hearts of our people and divided the time into "before" and "after." It is another proof that the purpose of this war is to annihilate the Ukrainians. How else can mass murder of unarmed people be explained? If the Russian invasion in February had shaken everyone, then what happened in Bucha became the point when resentment and hatred for the occupants reached a critical level. The words of the Ukrainian anthem became very relevant: "Our enemies will perish as a morning dew in the sun." All that could not but generate many questions and complaints to God. New circumstances arose that not only Ukrainians but the world had to understand and redefine. So, the "Theology After Bucha" conference was an international one, and its participants gathered together to discuss the context of the theological education in eastern Europe and Central Asia.

It is symbolic that the event took place in the Peace Hotel, even though during the nights while the conference was held the sirens sounded and some participants had to go to the bomb shelter at the Heroiv Dnipra subway station. Our Ukrainian soldiers who went through training also stayed at that hotel. Actually, it was because of those soldiers that I heard the Russian language for the first time since we had moved to Ivano-Frankivsk. Nobody speaks Russian in the west of Ukraine. But here, at the hotel, most of the military staff spoke Russian.

The conference became a place where we who were connected to Ukrainian seminaries could openly speak of our war experience, traumas, pain, and heavy losses. Of course, we found strength to tell about our hope for restoration, our willingness to serve our nation, and our anticipation of just peace.

It was clear to everyone that the seminaries had many difficulties as they found themselves in a new situation. The war put the educational process on hold, the number of students declined, teachers and leaders were exhausted. Besides, humanitarian projects had taken a lot of strength, and now, on the eve of the new academic year, the schools had to go back to educational activities. To make it possible, the participants discussed ways of partnering and promoting theological education.

Of course, the key issue was the way the theological education was to continue in light of the monstrosities our neighbor enemy committed among our people. As a means to illustrate, a trip to the campus of Ukrainian Evangelical Theological Seminary was organized. The campus suffered from the shelling of the Russians during their attack on Kyiv. There was still a lot of debris and broken glass there, and the cafeteria was damaged by numerous shells. A banner that had once greeted the students coming to study lay on the ground near the library. In the library, the staff created a war museum, placing fired cartridge cases and shells between the bookshelves.

As I was looking around the Ukrainian seminary, I could not but think how the TCI campus might look now. Russian troops had been there since March. We were informed many times that they kept taking things out of it. I was afraid to imagine how badly it was plundered. Years earlier, there was always an air of anticipation at our campus in August, as a new academic year was about to begin, and the students were coming to experience wonderful transformations in their lives. But now . . .

The conference participants also had the chance to visit Hostomel, Irpin, and Bucha—towns near Kyiv. Nobody will ever be able to express the sorrow and pain that befell their inhabitants. While I was there, I could not but think about my beloved Kherson. How are you, my city?

By the end of the conference, every participant realized its importance. Not only did it encourage the leaders of Christian seminaries and teachers, it also helped build a strategy for the future. Later, an official statement was issued by the participants of the conference. We all wanted to see theological education develop in our part of the world for the sake of God's kingdom and in order to meet the needs of our people. Now we understood what to expect. Besides continuing the work and meeting to strategize on how to promote education, we had to answer the questions of the people traumatized and scared by the war. Someone had to heal the scars left by the war. Perhaps we, theologians, were not able to stop the war physically. But we could bring some comfort to our nation, which the enemy caused to be disillusioned with God and mankind. We will not stop doing it even when the cannons are silenced, the enemy is defeated, and the long-awaited peace comes to our land.

As Chesterton has put it,* "At least five times . . . the Faith has to all appearance gone to the dogs. In each of these five cases it was the dog that died."

I want to believe that faith will triumph this time as well!

* Gilbert Keith Chesterton was an English writer, philosopher, and Christian apologist in the end of the nineteenth and the beginning of the twentieth centuries. The citation is taken from his work called *The Everlasting Man*.

Chapter 19

The Other Side of Volunteer Ministry

I DID NOT EXPECT THE VOLUNTEER with whom I was talking to open up so much.

"Although I have been in ministry for twenty years," he began, "I will not go back to being a pastor."

I must have looked surprised, but my interlocutor was not bothered by that. He continued, "I have become addicted to the ministry in which I bring rice, warm clothes, candles, and what-not to the people. I like it that they need me and thank me wholeheartedly. I need their response; it is like adrenaline to which I have become addicted."

Never before had I heard such a confession. The man was sharing with me something of which people usually avoid speaking. It felt like he wanted to add something else. He pointed to a small truck donated to us by our Dutch partners. Volunteers were carefully unloading the boxes with humanitarian aid. Mustering his courage, the man forced himself to say, "I can't even imagine being in your place. You distribute tons of humanitarian aid all around Ukraine and yet remain in the background. People don't even know about you, but I . . ."—he sighed heavily—"I need to see people's tears." He added after a short pause, "I even like taking pictures with them a little."

There were a lot of questions in my mind after our short conversation. The story of this pastor-volunteer is a vivid example of how one can get addicted to the gratitude of those who need you. This is a kind of messianism of our ministry.

I know by experience that during the first months of the war Ukrainians showed a great emotional response. There was nobody who would refuse to do, at least, something: to gather clothes and food, make candles, or weave camouflage nets. People responded to their emotions. That was the first wave of volunteers. But after three or four months, the number of workers decreased. It became clear that one needed teamwork and partnership in order to do a long-term ministry and avoid an emotional burnout. The man I talked to had neither. He is a living parable, a vivid example of the other side of volunteer ministry. I do not gloat; I am sorry for him. This addiction to adrenaline does harm mostly to him.

But there is the other side of volunteering that involves not only volunteers themselves but also those to whom they minister. I have already mentioned that humanitarian aid can "spoil" people. After volunteering for several months in a row, one can't help but notice how the receivers of the aid often become addicted to consumerism. And it can be very dangerous. Humanitarian aid can create a problem for suffering people in any part of the world by making them dependent on it. Helping a person out of a difficult situation, one can do him harm if he becomes addicted to a constant provision received from charities and to consumerism.

During World War II, the inhabitants of the Pacific islands often saw supply airdrops coming down from the sky and providing the US army with food, clothes, and other useful things. The soldiers generously shared all that with the indigenous population, not noticing that their kindness was having a negative effect on the latter. The limited worldview of the islanders did not allow them to understand the source from which the aid came. They started to believe that the help dropped from cargo planes was of a divine/miraculous nature. Just imagine for a moment how easy it was for the island tribes to give in to consumerism. Perhaps many of them stopped doing their habitual work, which helped them provide for their families. Even after the end of the war, the continuous anticipation of "the help from the sky" did not disappear in the southwestern Pacific. The islanders formed the so-called cargo cult.*

* "Cargo cult" is a term defining a number of religious movements on the Pacific islands. Using rituals, they try to re-create the maneuvers of American soldiers who were based in the southwestern Pacific during World War II and received a continuous provision that came from supply airdrops. After "white people" had left, participants of cargo cults continued to imitate the activities

Say what you like, but humanitarian aid weakens people.

Besides, it is important to understand that there is no such thing as free stuff in the world. Even the smallest humanitarian aid is obtained with the money that someone took out of his or her budget to help the needy. Sometimes it is a considerable sacrifice for a giver. I would not want the people of Ukraine to become consumerists. This is why a number of projects we did together with Dutch partners presupposed us giving our agrarians seeds that they could plant in the spring to reap a harvest in the fall. It was for the same reason that TCI focused on helping refugees get grants, which they could use to start small businesses and provide for themselves. This is what the Bible teaches us. Genesis starts with the description of how God worked for six days. When Adam was created, he was called to take care of the garden. Labor is not a curse, as some find it convenient to interpret the words the Creator said to the man after the latter had listened to the serpent. "All things are full of labor," Ecclesiastes says. "If any would not work, neither should he eat," Paul tells believers. It is not reasonable to see all these instructions and to provide a person with everything he needs without encouraging him to work. So, in our humanitarian projects we always tried to avoid tempting people with consumerism.

I know by experience what it means to lose everything and find oneself far away from home. I am familiar with the pain of my fellow citizens who suffer because of the war. I have heard how poor they became during the occupation. Many inhabitants of Kherson suffered but refused to make deals with the occupants: they would not receive humanitarian aid in exchange for a Russian passport. Some of them used up all their savings not to accept the "Russian Order." Now they have to ask for help—as embarrassing as it is for them (some of them were successful businessmen before the war)—and our responsibility is to lend a hand.

---

of the US army, making landing strips and planes out of tree branches to receive an abundance of heavenly gifts again.

Chapter 20

Conversation Without Masks

From time to time, I remembered our conversation with a man who had decided to step down from pastoral ministry to pursue mainly humanitarian projects. It was something to think about. One evening, as I was reflecting on our conversation, I received a phone call from Dick Alexander.

"Hey Valik, how are you?"—he asked me in his metallic voice. Dick usually used the shortened form of my name. We talked a little about our families. Betty, Dick's wife, has suffered from dementia for many years, which has taken its toll on his life as well. I have always marveled at Dick's resilience and really appreciate him taking the time to talk to me. Before the war, we used to try and call him once a month via video link to discuss things that were vitally important to me. Now our communication has become very rare, so every call from him has been a welcome one.

Pastor Dick Alexander is thirty years older than me. Today he is an elderly man. He is well into his seventies. He has given more than fifty years of his life to pastoral ministry. The fact that he underwent throat surgery for cancer has affected his voice—hence this metallic hoarseness in it. I cherish our friendship with him. It began in November 2007, when I had been the rector of the Tavriski Christian Institute for only about a year. During my first trip to America as rector, I was invited by Dick to visit a church in Cincinnati. I still remember that trip fondly—an unforgettable time! During the three days there, Dick gave me a special crash course in leadership and explained the peculiarities of American culture and American churches. Since our first meeting in Cincinnati, we have had many long conversations.

We have had several conversations already since the beginning of the war. Pastor Dick has always been interested in the challenges

I face in times of crisis. Each time, these conversations have been an important encouragement to me. Even now, I knew that our conversation would move casually into deeper topics that I dare not talk to many people about. But I deeply trust my friend and mentor Dick Alexander. He is an incredibly deep thinker compared to many Christian leaders. He doesn't settle for popular, trendy, and superficial things. I appreciate his ability to listen and then give a comprehensive but succinct answer, hitting the bull's-eye literally in a few words.

Since the beginning of the war, many foreign missions have been actively assisting Ukrainian organizations. Of all the organizations that actively donated money to humanitarian projects, only a few adhered to the principle of "don't let your left hand know what the right hand is doing"—that is, they did not demand reports or were careful about how to inform the public about projects that were implemented in a country at war.

I am fully aware of the importance of financial reporting. At TCI, we take these things seriously, but even though we have a department that covers our ministry on social media, there is some information we do not publish for two reasons. First, we filter what we publish in order not to frame people who live in the occupied territory or those who deliver aid to the danger zone. Second—and this is what has been on my mind lately—how do we strike a balance between the need to be accountable to donors, to involve new partners to humanitarian projects, and the desire to remain people who serve the community in humbleness and modesty? I don't know if it is possible to maintain this balance in the world of Instagram and Facebook, where fund-raising methods are crafted in accordance with modern marketing strategies.

In times of war, sensitivity to certain issues is multiplied manyfold. On the other hand, war destroys formalism in our hearts and forces us to reconsider our position on certain things we may have previously ignored. With economic problems and lack of resources, many issues we face in our lives remain unresolved.

Pastor Dick listened to me carefully. To help discuss my dilemmas, he suggested that I recall the facts that were bothering me.

I told him a young volunteer recently suggested that I enter his business project—the production of canned meat for the military at $2 per can, while the price of a similar product in grocery stores was $1 per can. I turned his offer down. He was annoyed and stated that we could ignore the inflated price and just slap the TCI logo on the product, which would serve as an advertisement on social networks. I find this approach extremely immoral. The second story I remembered was about how we evacuated a woman with three children. We were helping them find housing. After we announced the apartment search at a Sunday service, one family offered to provide an apartment to this family. However, just twenty days later, they called me and demanded that I evict the refugee family because they were considering new options for renting or selling their home. I begged them not to evict the family at least for a weekend, so that they could quietly attend a service at the church and move to a new place after the weekend. But my pleas proved futile, and the family was evicted on Saturday night.

During the war, a special term, "Facebook volunteer," was coined to refer to people who actively use social media to brag about the amount of work they do, and sometimes it's more pictures than actual work. I don't know what drives some of them to don body armor and helmets when they're two hundred kilometers away from the front line, just to look tough on the pictures and in their reports. Some of them spent a lot of money on their equipment, while there is not always adequate equipment for the military at the front. I noticed a similar approach in the work of some international organizations, which sent our reports back asking us to edit them. We were advised to use certain expressions that, in their opinion, would have a better impact on the emotions of their sponsors.

Dick listened to me and asked: "And how do you feel about that?"

I replied that I sometimes feel a strong emotional dilemma: The large number of projects, new partners, the people we help—are they not just numbers to me? I often ask myself a question, "Am I becoming just a church functionary? Am I becoming just a church official?" I am reminded of the words of the apostle Paul, who was pleased even with those who preached the gospel to aggravate his situation in prison. On the other hand, I remember the story of Ananias and Sapphira, which shows how corruption creeps into church society. I want to find a balance between the ministry and transparency. Is it still possible to publish our work on social media while maintaining simplicity, humility, and modesty?

Another challenge to face is my intense irritation that war brings the content of the human heart to the surface. I have seen Ukrainian women sell their hair and jewelry to help the military, while some volunteers reject accountability and spend the funds raised as they deem fit, sometimes in a way that is not transparent. I know several volunteers who forged documents just so they could cross the border, to never come back. Some of them forged their medical records; others got their travel permits as volunteers and never returned, violating the terms of their foreign travel permit. Some of them received significant financial support from international organizations, and the funds for the forged documents were extracted from humanitarian projects. That makes me angry.

"So how do you want the situation to change?" Dick asked me.

"Honestly, I don't know," I answered. "On the one hand, I would like us to retain our human side and remain humane even during the war, but on the other hand, I realize that the war has changed us forever. 'Not everyone of us will die, but we will all be changed' (1 Cor. 15:51 CEV)—these words were said by the apostle Paul; later they were echoed by Solzhenitsyn, speaking about the Soviet gulag, but they also apply to war. The war will not kill everyone, but it has already changed us all."

Pastor Dick listened to me carefully, thinking for a moment before answering. "This is truly a dilemma for a fund-raiser: How to remain a human being, remain a Christian, and still be effective in fund-raising? I realize that modern approaches to fund-raising can help raise more money for ministry, but it is important to remember that there are often manipulative elements in some of those methods. Without them, of course, effectiveness in fund-raising is diminished. Listen to what your heart guides you to do. From my experience, most organizations don't ask these questions. I have faced a similar dilemma myself and have found the answer for myself. I think you should make this decision on your own, too."

We said good-bye to each other and finished the call. The conversation helped me to make sense of my own feelings. I realize that the subject I raised continues to bother me, but now I have confidence that I can solve part of my dilemma. A metaphor came to my mind. I have often adhered to its wisdom in my ministry. There are two approaches in ministry, two opposing strategies. One is acting like a hunter. The hunter picks a moment and heads into the woods for prey, kills the animal, gets the meat. If one forest runs out of game, he moves on to other areas, seeks new places for hunting. The hunter's main criterion for success is quantity. He doesn't care about the ecosystem. The farmer, on the other hand, has a completely different approach. He puts years of work into creating an ecosystem where every bug, every blade of grass, every animal, bird, tree, or shrub is important. Over time, this entire ecosystem begins to bear fruit. Unfortunately, modern popular culture pushes us to measure performance only in quantitative terms. However, I believe it is more valuable to build and nurture an ecosystem that, in the long run, bears fruit.

I felt that I had resolved my inner struggle and was ready to go to bed. At that moment, a WhatsApp message came from a friend in Uzbekistan. It was about a student from Uzbekistan who had donated five hundred dollars to support humanitarian efforts in Ukraine. For me, this was confirmation that there is One who hears our prayers and responds to our dilemmas.

Chapter 21

New Academic Year

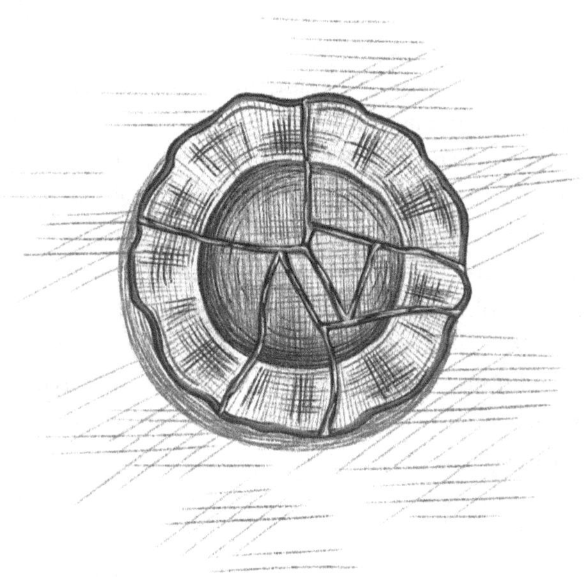

THE NAME OF OUR ORGANIZATION is still a reminder of where it was just six months ago. During that time, the Tavriski Christian Institute had to shift its focus to humanitarian projects, pushing its main mission—education—to the background. The usual educational process in which we had been involved for many years was now disrupted. While in western Ukraine, in Ivano-Frankivsk, we continued to reflect on our mission, occasionally discussing the possibility of starting the admission process for a new group of students. However, it was far from easy. We had to fight our way through the labyrinth of doubts, which every day stood before us like an impassable wall.

Will we be able to continue our work under the new conditions?

The war broke into Ukraine, crushing the usual peaceful life. It was unpredictable in its course; it kept taking more lives and made us live in fear. It caused harm even in those areas that shells or missiles did not reach—its threat was omnipresent. Civilians did not feel safe even far from the front.

How do we keep living in such conditions? How can we plan anything in such unpredictable circumstances? What to do when there are no guarantees and the contours of possibilities are barely visible?

We need huge reserves of moral and physical strength. We need confidence. But where do we find it?

The confidence in the need to admit a new class came to us gradually. The main impetus was that the war had awakened a great interest in spiritual matters, even among people who did not attend church often. We realized that it was important to satisfy this spiritual hunger. There was also a demand for theological education among those who were already in ministry. Pastors were eager to get a refresher training as the context of their ministry changed because of the war.

It has been a long time since I have seen such a strong interest in training among ministers. I was greatly encouraged by the opportunity to teach at a summer camp for pastors in Ivano-Frankivsk. This confirmed the need to open the doors of the institute to new students. In addition, society and the church were very optimistic as they saw the modest successes achieved by the Ukrainian army at the front. It seemed that a turning point in the course of the war was coming.

I will not go into the details of the usual preparations for the beginning of the school year. I should mention that the TCI staff had no opportunity to rest. Since March, the work of our institute has shifted to the humanitarian sphere. We simply did not have time for rest.

Sometimes living in overdrive was connected not only with lots of things to do but also with the acquired complex of guilt: you cannot afford to relax without an inner feeling of condemnation, because right now your fellow countrymen are under the occupier's fire. However, the batteries do need to be recharged.

In the first half of August, my team and I were able to get away to the Carpathians for a few days. This was all we could afford this summer. A month before the start of classes we had to reorganize our work, as we planned to return to academic activities. We planned that the academic process would take about 70 percent of our time.

Anyone who has experienced the start of a new school year in educational institutions knows that it is always an exciting time. While some disciplines may be somewhat similar in their content, each new year brings something unique with it.

However, the beginning of the 2022–2023 academic year was a particularly stressful time for us. We had to start teaching in a totally new environment. While our classrooms, buildings, library, and the entire campus in Kherson were fully prepared to receive students, here in Ivano-Frankivsk we had to start with finding a space that could be rented in order to launch the educational process.

We found a facility that had previously served as a hostel for students from India. There were no classrooms ready for classes in this building. Unlike our classrooms in Kherson, which had all kinds of teaching tools such as interactive whiteboards and projectors, here we had only white-walled rooms. We were able to purchase blackboards, chairs, and desks, but there was still the issue of equipment for students who had to study remotely. Some students who remained in the occupation planned to complete their studies. Fortunately, several organizations and churches came to our aid and helped us purchase the necessary equipment.

There were also difficulties with the library. We had to organize it in a small room on the second floor of the church building on Hordynskoho St. We had a larger library room even when TCI first started its work! Before the war the book fund of our institute in Kherson amounted to about thirty thousand copies, and now we barely had one thousand books.

I should mention that several Ukrainian seminaries contributed to our new library. When the news about the destruction of our institute's library by Russian occupation troops reached other seminaries, they each gave us from twenty to thirty theological books. Amazingly, two small parcels of books also came to us from Russia. One was sent by the staff of an Orthodox organization that opposed the Kremlin policies, while the other parcel came from an evangelical Christian. When he learned of our loss, he rushed to help. However, none of the Russian seminaries with which we had previously been affiliated in the EAAA offered support for TCI at this difficult time.

I have already mentioned our last prayer breakfast a month before the war began. One of our prayer requests was for the new class of students. That prayer came to my mind several times, and it seemed impossible to imagine then that TCI would be able to open its doors to students again. By the beginning of the school year, we had received about forty applications for the licensed program, about eighty enrolled in our online program, and another thirty joined our informal learning program. In addition, TCI was working to put together a professional development program for the pastors of the Ivano-Frankivsk region. We had some serious work to do in the coming school year.

According to our tradition, we planned to start the new academic year by getting to know our future students. Therefore, before the start of the first classes, on August 30, we held an online orientation session to get to know them better and answer their questions. Personally, I was deeply moved by this exchange, realizing the challenges that the TCI staff had to overcome over the past six months to see students who wanted to study theology again. This moment also took on a special significance because in those days the Ukrainian military was actively driving the Russian occupiers out of the villages on the western bank of the Kherson region, and there were periodic battles near Kherson. I knew from my parents and friends how badly the city was being shelled, how houses were being destroyed, how people were being killed. The news made me very worried. Early in the morning of August 29, I received a phone call informing me that the TCI base had been badly damaged overnight. Russian troops had been stationed there since March: they had looted and sold off our property, burned down the library, and now the sad news hit: three buildings on our campus had been destroyed.

Listening to our new students at this Zoom call, I could barely contain my emotions, constantly thinking about the destruction on the TCI campus. As I looked at our students, I was overwhelmed with joy, but on the other hand, I was still grappling with the reality of the destruction of the Kherson campus. I could barely contain my emotions and had to turn off the camera several times. What I did not realize is how intense the emotional pressure would become in just a few days, at the opening ceremony of the new academic year, 2022–2023!

We decided to hold it in the premises of the volunteer center Filter, as we did not have a suitable hall for celebrations in the room we rented.

I vividly remembered many of our celebrations to mark the beginning of the new school year. The upcoming school year would clearly be different from anything TCI had experienced in its decades of existence. Just recently, our faculty could not have imagined that it would be possible to teach students again. But here we are, starting the new academic year again!

It was not always easy for me to prepare for public speaking. I felt a little insecure as I wasn't sure I had prepared the right message. This year I was more anxious than usual. Sadness over our war losses had become an integral part of my life. I struggled to reconcile the joy of the beginning of the new academic year with the grief tearing our nation apart. After much thought, I decided to change the usual opening ritual. I used a symbol familiar to me from the Jewish culture. During solemn occasions, such as weddings, Jewish people break a glass to commemorate the destroyed temple. It seemed to me that the union of sadness and joy in this symbol is shown in its fullness. During my speech, I broke a beautiful plate bought in advance and called to honor the memory of Ukrainians brutally tortured to their death in Irpin, Hostomel, and Bucha.

After the festivities were over, I knew for sure that the day would come when we would glue the broken pieces together, according to a Japanese tradition (*kintsugi*), and work to rebuild what had been destroyed.

Chapter 22

The Twenty-Fifth Anniversary of Tavriski Christian Institute

I MENTIONED AT THE BEGINNING of the book that we had planned to celebrate TCI's twenty-fifth anniversary in the fall of 2022. We were in for a great time. Everyone was busy with the preparations for the festive and memorable event, and we began to get the campus ready well in advance.

The war broke into Ukraine and rudely overturned our plans. We had to leave our hometown in a hurry, settle in the west of the country, and watch with sadness how Russian troops occupied our campus. What had served for years as a base for theological education and ministry was taken away by the enemy overnight.

For many years we built buildings, improved the campus, equipped classrooms, bought books for the library, upgraded canteen equipment, bought sports equipment. The Russians looted everything: some of the books were burned; dishes from the canteen were used to pay for the services of women of easy virtue; Russian officers took the paintings from the canteen hall; they took computers and equipment and sent their loot to their relatives in Russia.

Is it possible to treat Russians as a fraternal nation after something like this?

Many ancient books portray a close but cunning neighbor as the symbol of perfidy, a friend who commits treacherous acts betraying other people's trust.

Never could we have imagined that such a future awaited TCI. The closer we got to the twenty-fifth anniversary, the more discouraging news came from Kherson. We were faced with a choice: to give up and give in or to pull ourselves together and celebrate an important event for the institute. The Old Testament story of the prophet Samuel served us as a good example. In a difficult time for his people, right in the middle of a war, he set up a stone, calling it Ebenezer, which means the "Stone of Help." The prophet defied the circumstances, as if to say, "Our struggle may not be over just yet, but we are still alive and plan to celebrate our small victories!"

That's why we decided to mark this milestone!

We used to celebrate the anniversary of TCI at five-year intervals. It always was a special event. When our institute turned ten years old, the celebration was held on a boat. Over the course of the evening, we sailed along the Dnieper River, then stopped on one of the islands, where a festive reception was held.

Our fifteenth anniversary was overshadowed by sad events: in 2012 many pastors in Central Asia were thrown behind bars. Despite this, we saw new avenues opening up for the ministry. It was during that period that our friendship with organizations that were important to us began. IDES, PBT, Johnson University, and Marked Men Ministries are all still in partnership with us today. Together with them we have started a sheep-wool-processing business in a Central Asian country; with some of our students we have started several sewing businesses organized as a ministry to rescue girls from sexual slavery and help sexual-abuse survivors.

To celebrate its twentieth anniversary, TCI gathered many guests from Central Asia and the Caucasus. The celebration was held on an outdoor terrace overlooking our majestic Dnieper River. The celebration concluded with a fund-raiser for the ministry to the Roma nation. These people (who have also sometimes been called Gypsies) did not yet have the gospel, and the PBT mission in conjunction with TCI was just beginning to work on translating the Scriptures for them. It was during those years that many pastors from Roma churches came to Kherson for training.

Now we were to celebrate our twenty-fifth anniversary in completely new conditions. For the first time we were going to mark this important milestone for us not at our campus, not on the bank of the Dnieper, but at a new place, no less picturesque, but still far away from home.

The usual tradition for us was to organize a conference on the eve of the event. We were trying to choose an important theme that could serve Ukraine in this difficult time and decided it would be good to highlight the dialogue between church and society. This is how the agenda of the scientific conference nation's theology was formed. We rented a large hall for the event at the Nadiya Hotel, which is very symbolic (*nadiya* is "hope" in Ukrainian). The festival was scheduled to take place on September 16 and 17. Liudmyla Filipovych from the Institute of Theology, Ukrainian Orthodox theologian Kyril Hovorun, German theologian Gottfried Sommer, and Marietta van der Tol from Oxford were invited as keynote speakers. There were also quite a few speakers from different parts of Ukraine besides these guests.

Surprisingly, the theme of the conference hit a nerve, considering all the events taking place at that time. For their part, the "Russian world" theologians pushed the Kremlin line that Ukraine was ruled by a "Nazi regime." We not only had to respond to this attack but also had to discuss the issues of our national identity, the responsibility of Christians to society, and the dialogue between the society and the state. After all, in the post-Soviet space, believers largely adhered to the concept that our residence is in heaven, nothing holds us back on Earth, and therefore the church should be careful in its relations with society, as its purpose is to admonish the world or to preach the gospel.

For a day and a half, conference participants examined tough issues from a variety of perspectives. Using examples from the Bible, the speakers helped us to see the concepts of historical experience and cultural context: nationality, citizenship, pacifism, defense of one's own home and people. Questions of culture and politics were raised. We discussed the role of language in a political and theological sense. Examples from history also showed how the church at different times has or has not supported the concepts of statehood and national identity.

The topics of the conference aroused genuine interest. Our students asked a lot of questions, and it was obvious that they were very concerned about what was happening in Ukraine. The conference participants included people of different Christian denominations, not only Baptists and Pentecostals, but also Orthodox and Greek Catholics. Even secular people showed interest. I particularly remember one participant. He was an employee of the Ivano-Frankivsk Philharmonic. He wanted to know the church's position on issues of culture, nationality, and citizenship, and whether the church and the people could defend their national identity in the context of war.

TCI also had a good opportunity to present several new books. This strongly emphasized the seriousness of our intentions in the projects we had undertaken before the war. Working with two publishing organizations, Tyndale House and LATM (Literature and Teaching Ministries), we translated books into Ukrainian. We found that there was very little theological literature for students in their native language. Now this work is even more in demand because the severance of links with Russia has made it impossible to import and use materials published in the Russian language, and students are increasingly interested in books in Ukrainian.

As we were preparing for the conference, we had no idea that it would also be a forum for the displaced people. Former Kherson residents, now living in Rivne, Lviv, and other cities in Ukraine, met and were able to have a frank conversation. This time was so special for those sharing similar challenges, because since the beginning of the war they had to face a reality that was nothing like their previous experiences. Their beliefs and their theology were put to a test. I observed that, despite their circumstances, they were as open with each other as possible and fearlessly raised profound questions. Back on February 23, 2022, these were very different people. The shock of war had disoriented them at first and put their faith to the test, but they had managed to rethink a few of their beliefs. It was clearly visible that this new life experience produced some significant results.

As the sounds of the conference died down, the twenty-fifth-anniversary celebration began, which culminated in a small reception. The arrival of friends from different countries was a special encouragement for us. It reminded us of the time after the collapse of the USSR, when many missionaries from the United States came to Ukraine to help our people in the development of church life. We greatly appreciate their contribution. We still maintain close friendships with some of those who worked in our region in 1991, 1995, and 1997. In our current situation, when Russians, who like to call themselves our "brothers," were looting even used mattresses and pillows from the TCI dorm, true friends have taken the time to come to Ukraine lending their support. It is worth mentioning a few of them by name.

In 1996, several pastors in Kherson who were seriously considering creating a regional Bible college for ministers reached out to a missionary from the United States who could help establish the institution. That missionary was Glen Elliott. Glen introduced the Kherson pastors to several Christian colleges from the United States. This is how TCI came into being. The bulk of organizational work fell on the shoulders of Glen (he was responsible for working with our American partners) and Mykola Balanenko (who handled administrative issues and communication with local government agencies). In 1999, the first national rector of TCI was elected, Pavlo Smoliakov. Pavlo started constructing buildings for the institute in 2004, after the purchase of a lot of land on the bank of the Dnieper. Since that time, the rectorship was taken up by a young minister, Serhiy Predit, who had recently returned from Romania after graduating from seminary. Due to his son's illness, Serhiy stepped down in 2006. The board of trustees first invited me to become interim rector, but over time it became a part of my life. We were so pleased to see that Glen Elliott, who stood at the origins of TCI, was able to come to our celebration.

Scott Weber was another special guest at the institute's anniversary. In 1997 he planted a church in Estes Park, Colorado. This congregation was invited to become a TCI partner, and shortly after that they offered their financial support. At that time, it was suggested that one church would commit to paying tuition for one student. It just so happened that the Estes Park church chose me as their student.

I remember that Scott Weber often visited Kherson. Members of his team helped Kherson churches with various construction projects. Scott also occasionally taught a course on the Epistle to the Romans at TCI. I became friends with Scott and turned to him for advice. I even remember our discussions about my prospects of working at TCI.

I also can't help but mention Steve White and Monty Smith, important guests at our celebration. Pastor Steve White has done much to develop the relationship between TCI and American churches. The story of Monty Smith, pastor of the church in North Syracuse, New York, could be told by the children from villages around Kherson where he conducted sports camps.

We all felt that the arrival of overseas guests for the twenty-fifth-anniversary celebration was a special treat. We had not received so many guests from abroad since the beginning of the war.

There were also Ukrainian friends who attended our event. One of them was Pavlo Smoliakov. Pavlo, as I already mentioned, was the first national rector of our Bible college, and he currently serves as a regional bishop in Kherson. Another guest was Serhiy Turkach, who in 2017 led TCI for six months while I was in training. There were also alumni now serving as pastors from all over Ukraine.

The visit of two rectors of the Odesa and Kremenchuk seminaries came as a surprise for TCI. This was a strong testimony for our small educational institution, which always tries to maintain friendly relations and is eager to develop strong partnerships with others. The two rectors—Oleksandr Geychenko and Ivan Ovcharenko—coauthored the letter "Standing Together with TCI," which was signed by five organizations and five seminaries. We appreciated the value of this gesture. My friend Taras Dyatlik, watching this initiative unfold, said that this was the first time in the twenty-five- or thirty-year history of theological education in Ukraine that seminary leaders have voiced their support out loud and asked Western partners to help TCI financially. Perhaps this will not happen again in the next thirty years.

When it was my turn to speak as rector, I had only to thank everyone for their participation and summarize all the warm and heartfelt things that had been said by others: "Before the war, I often taught students that their mission does not depend on infrastructure. Now that we have lost all our infrastructure, I realize that we must fulfill our mission regardless of where we live or what resources we have. But I'll tell you honestly, without infrastructure it is a much tougher challenge!"

As we listened to congratulatory speeches from guests and received feedback and gifts from students celebrating the twenty-fifth anniversary of the institute together, we wondered what the future would have in store for us.

Curiously, there were no air-raid or missile-strike sirens during those two days. Only in the evening, when the celebration was over, did the siren go off for the first time in a few days, warning that missiles were flying toward Ivano-Frankivsk. Fortunately, the Ukrainian air defense shot them down at a safe distance from the city.

This was a very emotional time for me and my colleagues at TCI, because it was only three weeks after the destruction of our campus in Kherson, with heavy fighting raging still around our hometown.

Chapter 23

Deformation

THE GUESTS LEFT. THE COLD, NASTY DAMPNESS of drizzling rain drove me back inside, into a warm room. I tried to read Orhan Pamuk's volume on Istanbul melancholy and realized that I was beginning to feel some signs of melancholy myself, bordering on depression. But why? Just yesterday we were celebrating our twenty-fifth anniversary, and today I feel that the highlights of celebration, the burst of emotions, the fireworks of colors that excited and mesmerized me the day before are completely gone. The flamboyant joy shrank to a microscopic spark glimmering deep in my soul. Joy yielded room to sadness, and this new lump began to grow inside of me. I realize that nothing good can come out of this—just depression. I felt this unpleasant feeling many times when a party was over and the next day of everyday life begins. This mood swing is especially unpleasant now, at the time of war. After all, sadness and sorrow, grief, and emotional tension in crisis situations never let you go. Light feelings and joy are transient and fade away so quickly.

This dull rainy day resonated even stronger in my soul this time because I will soon be traveling to the United States. For two weeks I will have to immerse myself in the American culture, face many bright and polite smiles, and I will have to smile back, talk about our ministry here . . . but what to do when on the inside there is absolutely no incentive or reason for joy. The war has taken its toll on us Ukrainians.

I don't know what tools professional therapists use to help those who experienced the hardships of war firsthand. We did not have the opportunity to dispatch a psychologist to everyone we bring from occupied territories. I can only state one thing: our people recovered on their own, as much as they could. A fair objection can be raised here: Did they really? Maybe under the constant stress of the war they just have to hide their emotions deeper. I don't know. We Ukrainians still have to live with it and deal with it. Maybe in the future we will have to train rehabilitation specialists and mental trauma therapists, but that is still in the future. Today we are what we are. That is why we need to have patience with one another, because everyone has had their own share of traumatic experiences, and they continue to live with it.

"I jumped up in horror!" says Vitaliy, a resettler from Kharkiv. "Are they really shelling us again?!"

It turned out that the utility workers had just dropped a heavy garbage bin outside. Even now, the man still suffers from panic attacks and insomnia. He's a law professor. He and his wife were forced to spend a week in a bomb shelter in their hometown of Saltivka (the largest residential neighborhood in Kharkiv), under artillery fire. At the first opportunity, they left, taking with them just their cat, leaving everything else behind.

"My mom stepped out of her house to visit her friends, and it saved her." Oleksandr, our student from Kherson, shares his painful memories. "A shell hit our apartment. Everything we've accumulated over the years was destroyed in a second."

These were the many horrific manifestations of the Russian world for many Ukrainians. Its influence is monstrously traumatizing, even if you observe it from a distance. The war taught me a lesson—people do break down and are much harder to fix than cars. I observed this in the lives of our students, whom we evacuated on the first day of the war. They lost their ability to rest. They could not read books, watch movies, or simply relax. Some could even do inappropriate things. War has a way of driving people crazy, literally. It is not something you want to get more of.

And yet there were those who were able to overcome their personal trauma, such as our student Nika.

"My dad died in a tank," she says calmly.

We didn't believe Nika would be able to recover from the loss of a loved one. But after a while she immersed herself in theology and hardly ever left the library. Studying became her coping mechanism.

When we were able to evacuate Maryna, my sister-in-law, from Nova Kakhovka, she walked in a bent position for two weeks—she was afraid of gunshots and explosions. It was impossible to look at her without sympathy. One would think that in a safe city, in a safe place, people would loosen up, shake off the oppressive experience. Maryna had to relearn to speak in full voice and walk with a straight back. It was the stamp of war. Maryna lived five kilometers away from the Kakhovka Hydroelectric Power Plant, which the Russians captured on the first day of the full-scale invasion. Not far from her home the Russians stationed multiple rocket launchers spewing thousands of deadly rounds.

How can something like this leave your soul unscathed?

I remember the emotional roller coaster when my wife and I received a message from Maryna: "Kakhovka is getting shelled!" It happened on the day when Pastor Yaroslav Kibit invited my wife and me for a short walk to the Volchenetsky Mountains near Ivano-Frankivsk. We could not stop thinking about Maryna and what she must have been going through.

How can we hike here in the mountains when the enemy artillery is wiping out apartment buildings?

We were tormented by pangs of guilt. For a long time, we could not allow ourselves any vacation as a family. Only many months later did we decide to force ourselves to get together on Saturdays and spend time as a family—such was the pressing reality of war.

Maryna had to live through some tough moments. As I mentioned, she was unable to evacuate with the TCI team in February 2022. She moved into the basement of a friend's house to help and support her elderly mother. This is where they spent the months of the occupation together, sheltering from shelling, sometimes surviving without food. Now Maryna is outside Ukraine. It was incredibly difficult for us to say good-bye to her. I remember the freezing rain on the day of her departure. We gave Maryna a ride to the Polish border. She was walking in the rain, stooping under the weight of her travel bags, as my wife and I stood helpless on the Ukrainian side of the border and could not help her in any way. The freezing rain amplified the crushing feeling of loss and separation. With every second it grew stronger and pulsated with the frightening thought—what if we'll never see each other again? What will happen to us? What will Maryna's life look like there? The grindstone of war rolled over her, crushing her to the point that it was hard to say whether she still believed in God.

On the other side of the border, Maryna met a woman who had come from the United States specifically to help those fleeing the war. Maryna always gets emotional when she tells how this American lady, a total stranger, gave her hot tea in a paper cup. In the difficult circumstances of life, such seemingly trivial things become something special and memorable because they are done with genuine support, care, and love.

Even for me, this case was a ray of sunshine on that rainy and damp day. I thought about this woman who had paid a lot of money to end up on the Polish-Ukrainian border, far away from her home, to greet refugees with hot tea in paper cups. Before the war I didn't understand why there was no mention of God in the book of Esther, which describes a difficult time for the nation of Israel. Looking at the sacrifice of this American lady, I realize: God is exactly where he was in the time of Esther, and he now helps Ukrainians today. I am reminded of Martin Luther's metaphor of God's fingers on Earth. This lady truly was his loving hand touching people in need.

Logically, those who managed to exfiltrate from the dangerous area need rest, recovery, hugs and understanding, a shoulder to cry on. Unfortunately, the situation in Ukraine does not provide such opportunities to everyone. Even being far away from the front, from the occupied areas, the weight of a zillion new things that need to be taken care of and new experiences typical of a refugee life get dropped on people like a slab of concrete. Such moments are usually filled with self-pity, grumbling, anger, and resentment, but does it really help? One has to gather the remaining strength to live on and face the challenges. "Dignity in hard times" is how Ernest Hemingway once characterized it. Yes, dignity! It manifests itself even in the smallest things. Everyone expresses it in different ways, wherever life may take them.

I recall another lady whom we evacuated from Kherson. She lived with us for some time in a three-room apartment. As a sign of gratitude, she started cooking delicious pies for our family every day. The filling was always different—she used onions and eggs, sometimes meat or potatoes.

"I cannot just sit on my hands," she said. "Let me do something for you!"

Later, the woman traveled through Romania and Spain to the United States. Her life is yet another page in the war book. It is filled with traumatizing experiences scribbled in scrawled letters. We often carried people to the border with nothing but small purses, realizing that they would probably never come back. At such moments I think that the war exposed our nerves to the point they are no longer under our skin, but on top of it—everything is so painfully sharpened. The prophet Jeremiah experienced similar pain in his life; that's why he said:

> Oh, that my head were a spring of water
> and my eyes a fountain of tears!
> I would weep day and night
> for the slain of my people. (9:1 NIV)

An interpreter who worked for Human Rights Watch to collect evidence of war crimes once told me that people who survived captivity tell more truthful facts about what happened to them in the first days after their release than they do afterward. There is some kind of internal protection that clicks in people's minds when they have to share (and relive) again some of the deprivations and humiliation that occurred during the period of imprisonment. Over time, the presentation of information becomes more attenuated. This is certainly not the notorious Stockholm syndrome, in which victims sympathize with their offenders, but some emotional deformation still takes place.

I encountered something similar when talking to a friend who had been in Russian captivity for almost a week; his memories changed and gradually became softer and softer with each passing month. It was as if the human brain was blocking access to the most brutal and truthful details, and every time a lighter version of the events came to the surface.

Many Ukrainians have paid a high price. An acquaintance of mine, Serhiy Boiko, had his son arrested by the occupiers. They kept him in captivity for several days. It sometimes seemed to me that this was a favorite practice of the Russian military: coercing civilians while holding their family member hostage. Oleksandr Babiychuk, executive director of the Ukrainian Bible Society, had his son kidnapped in the early days of the war. The Russians used this to put pressure on the father for a long time. Oleksandr's son was tortured in prison for many months, then thrown out of an FSB (Federal Security Service) car traveling at low speed. He was severely emaciated and had endured severe abuse. Roman Meshtanov found himself in similar circumstances. His father served in the Melitopol church and taught psychology at TCI; he also took part in our video production. One day the Russians came to a church service, arrested all the pastors, took their fingerprints and gave them twenty-four hours to leave the city. Roman was unable to leave with his father in time and spent ten days in detention. Only later was he able to evacuate to Poland, thanks to a woman who was able to save him from a second imprisonment. Who knows whether he would have survived it again.

Pastors and ministers of evangelical churches often found themselves in Russian captivity. They were often detained by the Russian military just because they were conducting worship services and providing humanitarian aid to the people. My father is a church pastor, and he often felt the pressure of the Russian occupying forces in Kherson. FSB officers came to him several times and demanded at gunpoint to reregister the church under the Russian law, or demanded that he tell them how his church received humanitarian aid and medicines. In the past, my father had experienced pressure from the Communists under the Soviet Union, so he reacted to the threats of the Russian military with complete calmness and continued his ministry in the church.

Businessmen also suffered from the arbitrariness of the occupation authorities. My acquaintance Vasyl Zyk had his entire agricultural business taken away by the Russians. He and his employees were held at gunpoint for seven or eight hours, which they spent lying on the ground. My aunt Lilia Proskurina spent four long months in Russian captivity. She was swept in for preparing lunches at a church that fed children. When the Russians invaded Ukraine, they started forcibly moving children to Russia under the guise of "taking them to a safer place from the war area." Sometimes entire orphanages were moved out. The "liberators" did not hesitate to take children from their families either. These deliberate actions were aimed at depopulating the occupied territories. Pastor Pavlo Smoliakov and the Golgotha Church in Kherson hid children from an orphanage in the basement of their church for a month. Doctors and nurses helped, taking turns on duty. My aunt helped to feed the children, many of whom were between one year old and five years old. Some of the collaborators reported to the occupation forces about the underground orphanage. The Russian military raided the church and took the children away. Lilia was accused of some terrible crimes and thrown into prison, where she spent several months.

Thinking about the emotional trauma suffered by Ukrainians, I am reminded of one of the books of the Bible that was also written in the middle of a war. It is the book of Isaiah. In it, the prophet reflects on the period after the war; he passionately longs to see the Lord deliver the people of Israel from pain, turmoil, and cruel slavery. I am sure many Ukrainians today are longing for the time when the war will end and hope that the time will come when our war wounds will heal.

Chapter 24

US Trip

Before the war, my international partnership activities included regular trips to the United States. Once a year, mostly in the fall, I attended the Mission Conference (ICOM) and met with partners, colleagues, and friends. This year may have been an exception. Ukraine imposed martial law. Now, during the war, foreign travel requires many government approvals. The schedule of my upcoming meetings has changed. If earlier I was dealing with education projects, now the main topic was helping my people.

My traditional schedule for an overseas trip usually looked as follows: I would leave Ukraine on Saturday to participate in a church service in the USA on Sunday, and then have two weeks full of meetings. This time the travel took one day longer than usual. We had to travel to Poland to fly to the United States from the Warsaw airport. My wife and I flew into Chicago on the Friday evening of October 21. We stayed at the Holiday Inn near the First Presbyterian Church of Evanston. We spent Saturday morning meeting with the missionary committee and representatives of the charity fund and then flew to Cincinnati, Ohio, at noon. My sister Tetiana was to join us there. She had been in Nebraska since August on a United for Ukraine program. During that time, she held a public auction where she sold her photos and raised funds to support Ukraine. We were to spend the rest of the trip across the United States with her.

We landed in Cincinnati. I had a lot of memories that linked me with this city. Some of the first American missionaries who came to us in Kherson in the early '90s were from Cincinnati. Later I visited this city many times myself and often stayed with the Shelleys. Barry and Barbara built a large farmhouse in the suburbs of the city about forty years ago. Over the years, Cincinnati grew so large that their house, with a fairly large plot of land, already was within the city limits.

I remember that very first time, in 2017, when the Shelley family invited my wife and me to visit their home. Barb taught us how to play the board game Settlers of Catan. Since then, we have often spent time with the family on the weekends playing this board game. Now, five years later, my wife and I are back visiting with the Shelley family.

For the first time since the beginning of the war, I felt almost at home. In the past eight months, I have never been able to feel like anything other than a displaced person in any house or apartment. It's such a strange feeling, born of war, when you think, "Maybe at least here I can feel at home." But when you realize that the town where your home is right now is far away from you, you know that you're not at home. Barb suggested that Luba and Tetiana cook a Ukrainian national dish. They decided to treat us to Ukrainian *varenyky* (pierogi) with cherries.

We planned our trip so that each meeting would be accompanied by a photo exhibition of Tetiana's work. We knew that her photos would help people to visualize what is happening in our country and join projects to help Ukrainians.

Tetiana has long been an avid photographer. I have already told you about her first photo exhibition, *The Story of One Kitchen*. In August, she traveled as a photojournalist to the long-suffering Donbas and the frontline town of Soledar. Her shots became part of a photo exhibition, which she now showed to Americans. She said the following about her trip to the front line:

> The war in Ukraine is the most documented one in modern human history. Over the centuries, journalists and laypeople have not had a chance to take so many photos and videos, conduct so many interviews, or collect so much documentary data as they have today. I didn't want to add my own work to this gloomy palette of destroyed buildings, ruins and faceless crowds of war-stricken people. I wanted to portray stories of specific people, to convey the pain and

> suffering of each individual: here is a woman whose cow was killed in the vegetable garden, and here is my grandfather—he lost his eyesight because he had to spend three months in a basement without light. When I found myself near Soledar among our military, I was touched by the conditions of their lives. Every now and then my camera captured impressive images of soldiers risking themselves, sacrificing everything they had to hold the front. Not having enough food for themselves, they feed dogs and cats abandoned by the residents. I felt their love for their people in everything they did.

Tetiana's photo exhibition proved to be a wonderful addition to the meetings where we told people about our nation. It became an important communication tool in our outreach effort. After all, news about the war in Ukraine was quickly forgotten. After one of our meetings at the Eastside Church, where we also held a photo exhibition, Tetiana and I were approached by a reporter from the local TV station Local 12. I saw a puzzled look on her face as I spoke about the events in Ukraine. She could not believe that what was happening to our people was so serious and that it was still happening right now. It became clear to me that by October 2022, the topic of the war in Ukraine had gradually disappeared from the front pages of the news. The photo exhibition helped us to remind people of the plight of Ukrainians. Each of her photos helped Tetiana achieve her main goal: to tell Americans that war is not just dry statistics of the number of people killed.

"Behind each photograph is a living person, as precious as any other human being living on Earth. The war has hit them hard."

We also brought a dozen Ukrainian flags to give as a keepsake to those organizations that have supported us throughout the war. Each yellow-and-blue banner had a thank-you signature left for them by resettlers, volunteers, and our soldiers. In each of my speeches, I thanked Americans for the assistance they provided to us during the evacuation and expressed my appreciation that their support continues.

After Cincinnati, all three of us traveled to the Indianapolis suburb of Plainfield to visit with Steve White. He had served as a senior pastor of the Plainfield Christian Church for many years. Now he focuses on developing partnerships between American churches and TCI. I must say that Steve's home changed my perception of American hospitality. It is worth telling a little more about how this happened.

In Indianapolis, we had a meeting with a classmate of mine from TCI. He was with his wife as well as his parents and his in-laws. We spent some time together. They shared stories of how they had to leave Ukraine because of the war. After socializing, we drove up to Steve and Diane White's house and got out of the cars to say goodbye. Steve suddenly appeared on the doorstep. Before we could say a word, he invited us all into the house—and there were nine of us! Diane began to set the table. As I knew from my fifteen years of visiting America, such a spontaneous gesture of hospitality was not typical of the local culture. Besides, hospitality through food is something that is more characteristic for Eastern cultures. This surprised not only me but also every Ukrainian at the White family table.

In Indianapolis, I had another unusual encounter with a man who twenty years ago was the deputy director of a Turkish school in Kherson. Somehow, he had learned that I was in town and had come to express sympathy on behalf of the Islamic community. Curiously, our meeting took place in the lobby of a Protestant church. He told me he could not fathom how the Orthodox Russians were able to wage war against a country that is also considered an Orthodox nation. I had not met this man previously. I was very pleased to spend some time with him. He told me about himself, how he was sent as a missionary from Turkey to develop the Islamic community in Kherson. We shared warm memories of our hometown.

Our work trip ended with the ICOM Missionary Conference in Columbus, Ohio. I was tasked to lead a workshop on the impact of war on missions in Ukraine. I spoke about the humanitarian projects led by churches. So many people came to the event that there were not enough seats. Some people were forced to stand in the doorway. I finished my presentation with a story about my grandfather Pavlo A. Syniy, a World War II survivor:

> I understand why my grandfather often told us the same stories about what happened to him. When he was a POW, he and other soldiers were transported through a German town. A middle-aged German woman asked a German convoy soldier: "May I give some bread and half a glass of milk to prisoner number 88?" The soldier allowed it. That #88 was my grandfather. Even fifty years after his liberation from the POW camp, he remembered this vividly and shared in detail about this act of kindness of a strange German lady. It was one of the highlights of the whole war for him, along with the story of liberating their camp when one of the British pilots gave him a bar of dark chocolate. Grandpa often said, "Can you imagine, a whole bar of dark chocolate!" At that time, it was impossible to find chocolate in Soviet grocery stores; it began to appear on the counters only when the USSR was on the verge of collapse.

I often heard these two stories from my grandfather as a child and wondered why he always repeated them. As an adult, I read articles on brain research and realized that in extreme conditions, people tend to remember something pleasant in order not to cause themselves additional pain reliving their terrible experiences.

I have shared these stories with you to show that now, when my nation is going through an extremely harsh period, the imprint of this war is bound to remain on each of us. But even after many years, we Ukrainians will remember the good that the world has done for us in a difficult time. So, I ask myself a question: What will I tell my grandchildren about the war? I know the answer: I will share the story of how the Poles, Romanians, and Moldovans opened their countries to my brothers and sisters, how they set up tents with hot coffee and sandwiches at the border. I'll talk about the Dutch farmers who sent us truckloads of potatoes, sugar, and flour. And, of course, I will share with my grandchildren about you Americans, how you raised money so we could get children and moms out of the occupation and away from the front lines.

My work meetings were coming to a close. From Columbus we traveled to visit my brothers and sisters in Nebraska with a two-day stopover at the Bettendorf Christian Church on the way. Long before my trip, I had been invited by the pastor of the Bridge City Church to preach for them. The pastor and I thought for a long time about what the American church would want to hear from a Ukrainian visitor and finally concluded that the topic "How the Heavenly Kingdom Manifests Itself on Earth" would be the most fitting. The service had a good response in the hearts of the congregation. That church was going through a series of leadership changes and a name change at the time.

I rarely get time to relax on trips like this, but this time I planned to visit my family. My two brothers and a sister have lived in Lincoln, Nebraska, for about twenty years. I have visited them several times over this period. In the spring, after the big war broke out, another brother of mine had to leave Ukraine. Then, saying good-bye to him, I had no idea that already in six months we would be able to see each other again. Now, when all the important events were already behind me, we came to visit Lincoln, which became the second home for my numerous relatives. It was nice to see that there was a small community of Ukrainians in town, and that once a week people gather in the square near the town hall to pray together. The meetings bring together not only those who attend evangelical churches but also Greek Catholics and even people who are not religious.

We arrived on November 9. Our flight back home was scheduled for November 14, and it seemed as if time had slowed down for these couple of days. The hassle was gone. We plunged into unending heartfelt conversations. We talked about the war and our families, shared openly about things that were important to us, and which I am not always willing to share with people who do not have similar experiences. You can be frank with your family and not be afraid they will judge you. These few wonderful days in a family atmosphere became a special outlet amid the crisis. It was especially valuable, since it was the first time in a long time that our extended family had gathered in such a large group. I was so reluctant to let anything distract me from this family time after being on the road for two weeks. But my work caught up with me. I had to take part in an important Zoom call.

Chapter 25

Night Zoom Call

When traveling, I don't usually join TCI Zoom calls, because this would create an additional burden for me. Because of the time difference, it is quite difficult to find and coordinate a time that suits all participants. I am glad that we have a good team, and my colleagues are doing fine without me. Despite the challenges presented by the war, the TCI team continues to work like a clock. However, on this trip I was forced to take part in a conversation with an initiative group working to create an alliance of theological seminaries in Ukraine, Moldova, and the Baltic states. The time of the Zoom call was very inconvenient for me—2 a.m., Nebraska time, when everyone in Nebraska was fast asleep. I was at my brother's house, and our conversation would have caused additional inconvenience to the household. But the conversation was important, and I couldn't help but join in.

Taras and Olha Dyatlik, Ivan Rusyn, Roman Soloviy, Oleksandr Geychenko, Ksenia Trofimchuk, and I were scheduled to take part in the meeting. Also, a longtime friend was supposed to join us on this call. Out of respect for him, I won't mention his name. He was heavily involved in theological education for a while, and not only in Ukraine but also in Russia and Central Asia. He was a research supervisor for some; for others he was just a friend.

It was surprising that he has not contacted Ukrainians since the beginning of the large-scale Russian aggression, and he has never once condemned the war crimes committed against our people. However, we have heard repeatedly that he calls Ukrainians to come to peace with Russian theologians. A frank conversation with him was called for. My colleagues and I were very worried about how our conversation would go. The war had already caused us to lose many contacts with people we had been in touch with for many years. We were hoping that we would be able to maintain our relationship with this friend.

I hardly had any sleep before the call. Half asleep, half awake, I kept going over possible scenarios for the upcoming conversation. I got out of bed fifteen minutes before the start of the call, went to the kitchen, brewed some coffee, and adjusted my headphones in advance so as to make as little noise as possible in order not to disturb my family. We agreed in advance that the meeting would be held in English. Because of the war, a lot of Ukrainians refused to use the Russian language, much like in Georgia, after Russia invaded the country in 2008, many Georgians stopped using the language of the aggressor.

The conversation started earlier than we had planned and lasted for two hours. We planned to talk about our position on the war. This was a very sensitive topic for every Ukrainian. Our people came face-to-face with the destructive nature of war: murder, rape, looting, violation of international law. Each of us was convinced: it is immoral and inhuman to justify war.

Our friend, however, believed that the Bible calls us to have a neutral stance on politics, matters of the state, and therefore, the war. He argued that war was a negative manifestation of politics, and it was difficult to determine who was right and who was wrong. In his opinion, the right thing to do was to take a neutral position, as Russian believers did, with whom Ukrainians have stopped communicating. He urged us to have a more open dialogue with such "neutral" Christians so that we would take the initiative in "rebuilding peace."

We were surprised by the position taken by our interlocutor. After all, he had witnessed the events of the war and heard the pain of Ukrainians on our Zoom calls. He knew about the work of the Ukrainian seminaries and the deaths of some of our staff. How could he then continue to proactively maintain relations with Russian seminaries that directly and openly justified the aggressor? How could he agree with and promote such a position of Russian churches and seminaries in the West? He took it even a step further and spoke of the need for Ukrainian Christians to reconcile with Russians, which essentially meant we should turn a blind eye to such a blatant justification of the war of aggression and all its horrors on the part of the Russian Christians.

What kind of reconciliation can we even talk about on those terms?!

We tried to use all logical arguments: there was no hint of regret on the part of the Russians. What kind of reconciliation can we talk about if there is no repentance, no remorse for the terrible crimes committed by the occupying forces? All this time we have heard nothing but excuses from Russian Christians: "This is the Kremlin's position, and we have nothing to do with it."

The conversation clarified positions and aggravated the situation even more: our interlocutor argued that Ukrainians bear part of the responsibility for the ruined relations with Russian Christians. The following was offered as an alibi for the Russians: "You don't fully understand their situation. Russian brothers are being persecuted. We do not need to be distracted with what is happening on Earth, we should all look for the kingdom of heaven."

The clock showed four in the morning. I began to realize that the two-hour conversation had led nowhere. Was it really worth it to continue, if we were insistently asked again and again to initiate the "reconciliation" with the Russians, even though they had no sign of repentance or regret, which, in fact, was tantamount to acquiescence to the official position of their state. I indicated my desire to end the conversation. Everyone on the call also agreed that continuing the conversation was pointless. I realized that it would be difficult for me to rest after such an intense debate. We began to wrap up the meeting. I heard from one of my colleagues: "Something is happening here in Kherson," but I was way too tired and did not pay attention to it.

I went to bed deeply disappointed by the call. I wondered what these "neutral Christians" would do if Ukraine survived this war. Half asleep, half awake, I had fragments of our Zoom call on continuous replay in my head. At some point, bits and pieces of other conversations began to intrude into my dream. It turned out that my ears were catching the agitated voices of my brother Dmytro and sister Tetiana, who were discussing something very loudly downstairs in the kitchen. Their voices were getting louder and more distinct. I heard two words repeated constantly: "liberation" and "Kherson." Finally, I woke up to the exuberating news: Kherson has been liberated!

I couldn't believe it. The news was so big that it shook me to the very core, especially after the disappointing conversation in the middle of the night. Without washing my face, I ran downstairs and into the kitchen. Luba, my wife, my sister Tetiana, my brother Dmytro, and his wife, Oksana—all of them were echoing with one voice that Kherson had been liberated!

"Is it true?" I asked in disbelief. "Couldn't it be some Russian disinfo?"

It was all over the news. I still couldn't believe my eyes and ears. I went back to the room to get my phone. More than fifty messages popped up on the screen. All of them were similar.

Congratulations, Kherson is free, again!

Chapter 26

Kherson Is Free!

The news was overwhelming. We started calling friends, eager to learn more details. The communication with Kherson was disrupted. Later we learned that the Russians had blown up most of the transformer substations while leaving. We could hardly get through to our parents; there was a weak Internet signal in their part of town. My mom confirmed that the city was indeed free, again!

We were speechless! We couldn't believe it!

Someone started dancing around the kitchen. Some couldn't hold back tears of joy!

My brother Dmytro suggested that tonight we have a family party. He decided to call all the family to his house and went shopping. I thought to myself that even last night we were arguing about peace on the terms of the victor, and here we were, a few hours later, celebrating the liberation of our hometown from the brutal Russian occupation. Of course, the liberation of one city does not equal peace.

We also called Stas, our younger brother. He informed us that a team of volunteers from TCI was already leaving Ivano-Frankivsk for Kherson.

Gradually, more and more reports and news about the liberation of Kherson came in. The first videos and photos of city residents welcoming Ukrainian soldiers on the streets appeared on the Internet. Soon the official authorities announced that Kherson had been returned to the control of the Ukrainian government. Cars flying Ukrainian flags filled the city streets.

We observed Kherson residents gathering downtown, on the Svobody Square. The events of March 2022 were still fresh in our minds when Russian soldiers dispersed local protesters on this very square with flash-bang grenades and shots in the air. The world saw footage of Ukrainians standing with yellow-and-blue flags and "Go home!" placards addressed to the occupiers. Now, looking at the footage of these men and women crying with happiness, we of course shared their joy of liberation. Our city was under the Russian occupation for nine long months. It was a time filled with fear, pain, uncertainty, and turmoil. The hope for the liberation of Kherson was alive in the hearts of those who stayed and those who were forced to leave the city.

Now, finally, the news that our hometown Kherson is free resonated with each of us! We were so happy to see Ukrainian flags raised above the buildings!

Dmytro came home an hour later. He brought several bags of food for a festive dinner. Soon, relatives began to arrive at my brother's house. I remember that there were so many people gathered that it was absolutely impossible to find a place to sit down. People even ate standing up or on the go. Everyone was constantly moving from the dining room to the hall, watching the news, loudly discussing every new detail. I received congratulatory messages and calls from different parts of the world.

The liberation of Kherson is undoubtedly the main event of the 261st day of the full-scale invasion of our country by the Russians. It is indeed the most joyful day in recent times. To be honest, I can't even tell when I was happier—on the day of my wedding, on the day my children were born, or on the day Kherson was liberated. You prepare for the wedding day and have some expectations that get built up to this happy event, just as you expect the birth of your children. But this time everything occurred unexpectedly, at least to us. We knew about the beginning of the counteroffensive of the Ukrainian Armed Forces in the south firsthand. It had been going on since the end of August. We were disturbed by the news about the destruction of the TCI property at that time. Since then, the events around Kherson have kept everyone in suspense for more than two months. The active fighting prompted the residents to evacuate—our volunteers once again had more things to take care of as they started moving people out. At the end of September, the Russian occupying forces held their kangaroo referenda on joining the Russian Federation in several regions of Ukraine they had previously occupied, but the air was filled with anticipation of the outcome. For nine months, the residents had grown weary of being under the occupation, and the constant fighting around the city had fueled their hopes for a speedy liberation. Everyone was worried: what if the Russians lured our troops into the city, with subsequent home-to-home fighting, which would inevitably lead to unthinkable civilian casualties and the destruction of houses.

I was very worried about my family and friends. And now, the long-awaited miracle!—I couldn't even believe it—it was like a bolt of thunder from a clear sky—Kherson was liberated! My brother's house was filled with joy and celebration. It is impossible to convey the emotions that filled our hearts to the brim. We congratulated each other. We sang Ukrainian songs. We thanked God!

The event gave me hope in a way I had never experienced before. I hugged my wife and told her that I wanted to fly home right away. Naturally, it would have been difficult for us to change our plane tickets. We stayed with our relatives for a few more days, and then on the way home we visited Luba's sister Maryna in New York State.

Maryna has changed so much since we said good-bye to her at the Polish border. Here in the United States, Maryna got married. Things had gotten better for her. Now she lived far away from the war. Although I still remember with pain the time when Maryna walked for weeks, ducking to the ground, after we evacuated her. It was impossible to forget the sadness we all felt as she left us, walking through the cold rain into the frightening unknown. Now she had hope in her eyes. So did Luba and I, for we were returning to Ukraine with a completely different feeling compared to the time when we flew to America. We were coming home!

I realize that for the past nine months I have been away from my home, the home that Luba and I have lived in for over twenty years. It's been taken away from me. But during that time, the whole country has become my home. I'm happy to be back. Maybe there was still a touch of sadness because I realized that I cannot go back in time, to my home, to the fellowship with the people I loved and spent time with. Just as it is impossible for most of my friends and relatives to return to Ukraine. But I was coming home, to my homeland, as it continues to fight for its freedom against the ruthless and bloodthirsty empire that is trying to steal home from every Ukrainian.

Chapter 27

Homecoming

As soon as I returned from my business trip, I decided to go to Kherson. I couldn't wait to be there. I was going to be part of a team of volunteers. For nine long months TCI maintained relationships with the people of Kherson, churches, and volunteers. When the occupation ended, our staff entered their hometown among the first volunteers. We were in a hurry to deliver humanitarian cargo in several cars. Another car from Transcarpathia was to join us on the way. They had to cover about nine hundred kilometers in one day.

I was sitting in a van, with my younger brother Stas at the wheel. I don't know how many such trips he has made. Sometimes it seems that since the day we set off for the evacuation, Stas has never stopped driving—he was always on the road: taking something one way, picking someone up on the return trip.

I looked at the November landscape on our way. Everything reminded me of the events of our February evacuation to Ivano-Frankivsk. I was glad that Kherson had been liberated. But somehow, as it had during the evacuation, a feeling of disorientation arose inside. It was a bit disconcerting: after all, I was on the way to my hometown. I've lived there all my life. But my heart told me that the war had stolen my homeland, my home, from me, and that we would see an entirely different city when we got there.

The prewar Kherson lives only in my memory now, and perhaps I will never return to that city, with those people, with those friendships and relationships—the war has permanently deprived me of it all. Realizing this, I sat quietly most of the way. Besides me and Stas, there were Vitaliy Mariukhno, Mykola Horodetskyi, and Kateryna Hatsenko in the van. But I realized that if I started to speak about the things gnawing my heart these nine months, none of my companions would judge me.

They all lived through similar experiences. Mykola, for example, had spent several months in the occupation. Kateryna, in her young years, had also experienced what it was like to be away from home (I have already told you her story, and how TCI helped her buy a violin).

Transcarpathian volunteers joined our humanitarian convoy at one of the planned stops. Now the team consisted of ten people. It is always a joy to see and realize that many of the burdens of war rest on the shoulders of such ordinary people who have dedicated their lives to volunteer work.

"Ukrainians must have become the most nomadic nation in the world in recent times," someone said as I was deep in my thoughts.

"Indeed, the war has forced our people to travel more often," said another, "although there is little good in such travels when we are forced to leave our homes to find ourselves in another part of the country."

"Ukrainians are discovering Ukraine. After all, humanitarian cargos, volunteers, chaplains travel on these roads every day."

"What else does a Cossack need? Freedom!"

I decided to support the conversation: "I agree, the ability to move wherever you want is a valuable part of freedom."

For a moment I also thought that the war unleashed by the Kremlin is also an attack on our freedom: the "denazification" is really an attempt to erase our national identity, and the "demilitarization" is required so we can no longer defend our freedom, as our army does today at the front.

We did not encounter any checkpoints almost the entire way from Ivano-Frankivsk. We were stopped only at the entrance to the Mykolayiv region. Studying our passports, which usually have a stamp with the place of residence, the soldiers asked us: "So you are going back home to Kherson?"

"Yes!"

Seeing how our eyes lit up with happiness, the soldier warned us: "You will not be allowed in before 6 a.m. The entry will be closed till then."

"We'll just wait in Mykolayiv then."

We reached Mykolayiv at three o'clock in the morning. We stopped near the church pastored by Oleksandr Rudenko. We did not dare to wake up the resting custodians, realizing that the people might have had a lot of work to do during the day. We slept in the cars. Only closer to six did we dare to disturb them. A volunteer showed up at the door; he was also a deacon of the church (I knew him—he was a TCI alumnus). When he saw us, he said we should have called them in advance. We made our way to the church cafeteria. There were several women there already cooking food. They gave us sandwiches, and one of the ministers made us coffee. We had a quick snack and hurried to get back on the road.

Autumn dawn lit the dull steppe landscapes. I realized that I had not seen the steppes of my homeland for the last nine months and had already gotten used to the mountainous landscape of Prykarpattia. I remembered a man I once met who had lived in the desert all his life. He spoke about the beauty of the desert with such enthusiasm. I was experiencing something similar. I really missed the yellow-brown colors of my native Kherson region in the west.

Our convoy sped toward the rising sun. The day was getting brighter. My eyes no longer had to strain to read the numerous signs warning "MINEFIELD." I was amazed at how many of them had sprung up here in a short time. Several times we had to turn off the pavement onto a dirt road to bypass blown bridges and overpasses. Every now and then we came across burned armored personnel carriers and vehicles—signs of recent battles. As we drove past one of the charred vehicles, I remembered a heartbreaking story an acquaintance had told me. Amid the Russian offensive on Mykolayiv, he was on the road when one painfully familiar car caught his eye among other vehicles that had been hit. The man parked by the roadside and found in the burnt-out car the charred body of his friend, who had died in the shelling. How hard it is to come face-to-face with the grin of war and helplessly watch as it mercilessly takes away your close friends.

As we moved forward, we saw houses destroyed by enemy shelling. It was not a pleasant sight to see the ugly remains of once-beautiful buildings. Someone had lived there; invested their efforts, time, and resources; made it comfortable for their family; raised children; planned to grow old there—but the invaders came and destroyed everything overnight. Today numerous settlements were turned into ghost towns: broken walls, empty windows, blown-off roofs, huge holes gaping in the fences—signs of the horrors of war.

The Chornobaivka airport was already seen in the distance. I remembered how we picked up very young recruits here in February to take them to Mykolaiv. The sight of the destroyed airport pricked my heart with a sharp needle. How much it had suffered under the occupation. Russian troops had seized it at the very beginning of the invasion. But they were never able to make full use of it. According to some estimates, Ukrainian troops hit and destroyed Russian equipment and servicemen at the airfield at least twenty-five times.

On the highway near the turn to the airport we stopped at a Kherson checkpoint. In most of Ukraine, checkpoints are only manned at night. Closer to the front line, they operate around the clock—for entry and exit. The military checked our documents. They didn't have too many questions for us, Kherson residents. We decided to treat our soldiers to something tasty and left them a box of croissants.

I remember stopping briefly at the monument at the entrance to Kherson. We took a few pictures at the columns. I took pictures without pleasure. I can't explain this feeling. Perhaps, I didn't want to see in the photos the sad Kherson defaced by the war, or maybe because I decided to come to the city as an ordinary citizen who didn't need to be photographed at every step.

By eight in the morning, our humanitarian convoy of three cars was entering Kherson. I did not expect to find it full of life, as it had been in the past. I imagined that we would enter a dormant city. Never, in all my forty-odd years, had I seen Kherson so empty and deserted. It was a ghost city.

CHAPTER 27

At the entrance to the city, I could see a blown-up four-story store building. I remembered that before the war they sold computers here. The parking lot was always full of cars and shoppers. Now there was sullen, dead silence—a hallmark of a city that has survived the war. Farther down the road we came across destroyed buildings and trees with broken trunks and branches—the result of shelling. On the streets everything looked abandoned and deserted. Skinny dogs were sniffing around. Despite the sunny morning, the city seemed cloudy and cold. My heart ached at what my native Kherson had become during the months of the occupation. I wanted to drive around the entire city at once that morning to see all the changes that had taken place during the occupation, but such a trip awaited me later. First, our humanitarian route led us to the place where help was needed—my father's church.

One way or another, I was back in my hometown! My wish had come true! I looked avidly at the familiar streets, taking note of even the slightest change in their appearance. I incessantly compared the city with the prewar image that remained in my memory. I felt compassion, infinite compassion for everything I saw as we drove by.

The ten-minute drive through the city was coming to an end. From a distance, I tried to see the church building where my father served as pastor. That was where we were taking the humanitarian cargo. I must admit that after seeing the streets, I did not expect to find the entire landing near the church filled with people. There were about a hundred of them. We stopped in a parking lot between the church and two apartment buildings.

Stas jumped out of the cab and immediately started unloading the humanitarian aid. I got out and headed toward the church. I greeted the people. I looked at their faces and saw that each of them had something noticeably different about it. I had heard many times before that a person who has been through occupation can be easily recognized by the deep marks of stress, suffering, and fatigue. I saw that almost none of the people were smiling; their faces were sullen and tensed, as if reflecting their inner struggle and emotional pain.

I could also see sadness and loss in their eyes. Many people have lost the easygoing nature that was always characteristic for Khersonians before the occupation. They used to enjoy life and joke a lot—a typically southern trait. My fellow countrymen have always had a sense of humor and self-irony. Perhaps this is a consequence of a long history of coexistence with the Jewish diaspora, which has lived here for many years. Oh, how I would love to see this Khersonian gleam of joy in their eyes and hear their sparkling jokes again!

I also noticed the posture of these people. Many of them were slouching slightly. This reminded me of encounters with displaced people coming from other regions of Ukraine who had survived the shelling and often had to hide in bomb shelters. The conditions that the residents of Kherson had to endure became clear.

Now they were brought to the church by their need. Some came to replenish their supply of potable water, others came to get groceries, but there was no doubt that all these people needed support and fellowship. The church became one of the few places in the city where people found fellowship. Of course, there were other places in town where people could flock to socialize and exchange news, but the church was the oasis that proved to be sought the most. It filled people's physical needs and provided emotional and spiritual support. Seeing this made me realize even more that my decision to be here, first and foremost as a human being, was the right one.

"Hello, Son!" suddenly came a hoarse male voice. "How are you?"

I turned around. I saw my father looking very tired and gaunt. He had suffered from insomnia for the last forty-five years, and for that reason he often looked like that in the morning. Now his condition was further exacerbated by his battle with cancer.

We hugged each other quickly. At that moment, one of the people in need also approached my father.

"I'm sorry, Son, I must go." My father left me alone in the parking lot.

Of course, I'd really like to spend more time with him right now. He didn't need to explain the reasons he had to go. I realized that many of the people who had come here needed the pastor's attention, his wise counsel and spiritual support. I did not insist. All this overload of charity projects was created by the war, and the fact that relatives do not have time to communicate with one another—being deprived of this simple human joy—is also the new reality of the war.

A minute later I saw my mom, her eyes shining with boundless joy and tears streaming down her cheeks. We hugged warmly and walked into the church building. My mom shared the latest news and told me about my father: he was busy every day in the ministry and was still struggling with the progression of his illness.

Our conversation was interrupted every now and then as people came up to my mom with various questions, and she tried to pay attention to everyone. Almost all these people were new to the church. I was surprised to see so many. Even though many church members had left the city because of the war, the church was not empty. The time of occupation had encouraged other people to seek help in the church. Now, seeing all these new people in the church made me appreciate even more the importance of my father's work under the occupation. He stood firm and did not break under the pressure of the FSB and Russian officers. His example evokes the deepest respect: he stayed behind serving the people all this time. I reflected on my father. It occurred to me that perhaps he felt abandoned by his children, as he stayed in Kherson with our mother. All the children had moved away. Some did so twenty years ago; others, like my brother and me—because of the war—this year. Perhaps that is why serving people has become his main occupation, where he feels acceptance and can realize his potential. There was so much I wanted to tell him to cheer him up. I wanted to show him that his whole family is very proud of him.

Time flew by. My mom and I agreed that I would come to their place for the night. I had to visit my friends and acquaintances during the day, get to the TCI campus, and then finally come home. Stas and I drove around town. I kept looking at the liberated Kherson. I could not help but notice how impoverished the inhabitants were. They did not sell their homeland for a few Russian rations of humanitarian aid. I can imagine the delight and pride with which they pulled out their Ukrainian flags when the occupiers left the city.

I came to the store to see my friend Serhiy Boiko. He had experienced the full brunt of the occupation. I remember well how worried we were for Serhiy when his youngest son was taken into custody by the Russian special services. The reason was that his son was talking to a friend in his native Ukrainian language. It took Serhiy all night to search for his son. He found him only in the morning, at one of the police stations, and was able to rescue him from the Russian captivity. It was a dangerous time in the city—many people went missing.

Despite the difficulties, Serhiy not only survived but he was also able to find opportunities and help many people in town. I have already shared the story of how he became one of the key people through whom TCI helped the people of Kherson. I really value my friendship with Serhiy. He is the kind of friend you can talk with about any topic without masks, and when you need to, you can just sit together and be quiet for a while.

I also took the time to meet with Yakiv Savenko. He is the pastor of the Kherson Christian Church. Our warm conversation took place in the church yard. The day before, the entire residential neighborhood had been shelled with fragmentation shells. I saw that the ground was strewn with small metal flechettes about 1.5 inches long. The mere sight of these deadly projectiles sent chills down my spine. It is scary to think that one round can kill dozens of people. Yakiv told me that the other day mortars hit a neighboring house. I was once again horrified by the reality of everyday life in Kherson.

During our short meeting, Yakiv and I had time to reminisce about our days of working together at TCI. Yakiv worked in our student department for a long time. Now he, like my father, serves the people of Kherson. After the de-occupation of Kherson, churches suffered from a critical shortage of ministers. I also remember Yakiv's words of encouragement. He said as we parted that the day would come and we would rebuild TCI. We hugged each other. His encouragement touched me, especially since I would soon have to go to the campus to see the extent of the destruction with my own eyes.

We came to the central square in the heart of Kherson. Stas went for a cup of coffee with someone he knew, while I decided to walk around a bit. I had already noticed before that the stores and small bazaars were closed. One or two cafés were open. They were clearly operating at a loss right now. I heard that the owners had run them to at least give some outlet for the residents. When we were driving along the Mykolayiv highway, I saw a banner at a gas station that Ukrainian military personnel were offered free coffee.

Even from afar I saw two large tents with humming generators near the monument to the Heroes of the Heavenly Hundred and decided to go to that place. I knew that because of the critical situation with electricity in the city, the civil-military administration set up "The Invincible" tents. This was important for Kherson. The city had not yet recovered from the plunder of the Russian army. The noise of generators could be heard everywhere, and the air was filled with the smell of diesel. I walked toward the tents. Such places were always crowded, and you could count on seeing someone you knew there. I was pleased to mix with the locals who came here to recharge their phones and power banks.

I was surprised to see that the Russians had not touched the monument to the Heroes of the Heavenly Hundred during the occupation. It has been standing here since 2014 and was dedicated to the heroes killed by the Berkut riot police during the Revolution of Dignity, when members of riot police shot more than a hundred people during the protest in Kyiv. To commemorate the victory of the Revolution of Dignity, the people of Kherson demolished the Lenin monument standing on this spot and erected a monument to our national heroes. That is why I was surprised that even after the nine-month occupation it remained untouched, although the Russians were known to eradicate anything that had to do with Ukrainian history or our struggle for independence.

"Valentyn," someone suddenly called out to me. "Is that you?"

I saw a road bike on the path and a man lying on the green lawn. I turned around. It was Pavlo Stepanets. We'd been friends for years, and it was such a pleasant surprise to meet him here in his hometown, especially since Pavlo, a Kherson native, had moved to Kyiv a few years ago.

Pavlo said that after the liberation of Kherson he came back here on purpose to help the locals. He was mainly involved with the elderly: he helped them carry heavy bags with groceries, bought food for their pets. Pointing to his bicycle, Pavlo shared his new hobby: "In recent years I enjoyed traveling by bicycle."

Our communication was brief. Stas called and told me that he was coming up to the square. We hugged with Pavlo.

The Svobody Square was left behind. We were heading toward Antonivka, where the TCI campus is located. The streets where I used to walk as a child flashed before me. My youth passed here. I grew older, got married, and started a family. I found my calling. And all that was here—in Kherson! I felt my heart beating with compassion for my hometown. I saw the city, all wounded and battered. It looked completely different from how I always remembered it. Some of the roads were mined. Bridges got blown up. Houses were destroyed and burned. The occupiers have retreated, but they continue to constantly shell the city from the other bank of the river. But Kherson is free and lives on, despite the circumstances! Its residents have stood their ground. Even though they are still without communication, heat, water, and power, they will endure these hardships. I realize with sadness and grief that these war wounds will take a long time to heal. Perhaps, as long as the witnesses of this nine-month nightmare live.

Chapter 28

Abandoned Campus

THE ANTONIVKA VILLAGE IS LOCATED on the right bank of the Dnieper, in the suburbs of Kherson. This settlement merged with the city long ago. Our van was on its way there, to the TCI campus. To enter Antonivka, we had to go through a series of concrete vehicle traps. Not so long ago, it was a Russian military checkpoint. They controlled the entrance and exit to the highway bridge that connected Kherson with the left bank of the Dnieper. The bridge itself, known as the Antonivka Bridge, was now a pitiful sight: several spans had collapsed into the river. Even then it was not safe to be near the bridge. The locals warned us that the Russians frequently shelled this location from the occupied left bank. We sped through this dangerous section.

We saw destroyed tanks and charred hulks of military vehicles at the entrance to the village. Everything indicated that it was the place of recent hot battles. We saw houses that had been hit by artillery. My anxiety grew as we approached our base. Even though I knew in detail what it might look like then, after Russian troops had been stationed there, I was still worried.

Ivan Slobodian, a volunteer pastor from the Ivano-Frankivsk region, came with us. He actively helped us in the evacuation and continued to work with TCI for nine months afterward. I also called Oleh Derkachenko, a local pastor and former TCI staff member, and asked him to accompany us around the area. Oleh had been keeping an eye on the campus since February and had witnessed its seizure by the Russian occupation forces.

Here is the entrance to TCI. The main gate (we called it the "upper gate") is closed. We were warned: under no circumstances should we try to open it, as it might be mined. The lower gate stood wide open as we drove in. To protect the car from the snipers watching on the opposite bank of the river, we parked it behind the "Christmas Tree Building." This was the local moniker of a student dorm that had to do with its architectural peculiarities: each room of this townhouse-type building was built diagonally to its median axis and had its own outside exit, so it resembled a Christmas tree.

I got out of the van. The first thing I saw were three spent shell casings from 152-millimeter rounds lying right by the entrance. One such shell casing was half my height. There were also empty artillery shell boxes piled in the dried grass.

I heard the noise of an approaching car. It was Oleh Derkachenko, and Anatoly, our custodian. Anatoly had faithfully guarded our campus until the last moment, when the Russians ordered him not to show his face on the campus anymore. We hugged and greeted each other. Together with Oleh and Anatoly we walked along the paths of our institute. We had to follow the recommendations of the Ukrainian army: stay on the paths, do not pick up anything from the ground, do not approach strange-looking objects, do not enter destroyed buildings—booby traps and trip wires could be anywhere.

As we walked around the campus, Anatoly shared his occupation stories. One episode that is particularly seared in my memory was about a Russian soldier who volunteered to go to the front. The most shocking thing was that he was a member of an evangelical church in Russia. This "believer" stole a Bible from my office and went to TCI custodians every night to preach to them about God. That is, during the day he would commit war crimes, and afterward he would show up toting my Bible in his hand lecturing Anatoly and other staff members how to believe in God. This soldier kept emphasizing that the only correct version of the Bible was the Russian Synodal translation.

I wonder why, calling himself a believer, this soldier is not at all concerned that he and his compatriots are doing evil in a foreign country. After all, they cannot help but notice that their presence here is not welcome.

As I listened to Anatoly, I also remembered a story of a pastor from Kherson. Two Russian soldiers came to his church. After the service, they informed the pastor that they were also Baptist believers and asked him to give them communion. The pastor looked at the young men in amazement. These soldiers had come to kill us, had taken over our city, and without any reproach in their hearts, they so casually showed up for a private communion service. The pastor refused the Russian occupiers.

As we talked, we reached the administration building. One section of it was still standing. We thought it was safe to explore some of the offices a little. I stopped near the former reception area and thought for a while. I remembered how secretaries used to accept documents from students here. I peeked into the empty, looted accounting office. "There's nothing left," Oleh Derkachenko said. "The Russians have plundered everything!" His words echoed in my ears—"They plundered everything!"

As much as I tried to get into my office, I couldn't. Because of the explosion of the building, it was blocked with debris.

"There's nothing there," Oleh said sadly. "The soldiers even tore the linoleum from the floor, pierced the walls. Apparently they were looking for a safe with money."

We were genuinely surprised by this because TCI had never been a rich organization.

I recalled the cozy furniture in my office and a beautiful collection of souvenirs on the shelves brought from foreign trips or presented by our partners. A round table for meetings in the middle of the room. Two desks by the windows: mine and my colleague Leonid's. There were paintings hanging on the walls, of which I often told my guests: "These three paintings reflect my theology: redemption through Christ, servant leadership, and the theology of hope." On the left side of the table hung the painting *The Lighthouse of Hope*, a treasured gift from the Plainfield church in Indiana. The wall on the right was decorated with a painting by Serhiy Kober featuring Christ washing Peter's feet, given to me by the Wycliffe Mission staff from

Britain. And opposite my desk on the wall there was a two-picture composition painted by Lena Navarro (my brother's sister-in-law): Christ's pierced feet and hands as a symbol of our redemption.

"That's a shame, those were beautiful paintings," I said sadly to my colleagues who were with me at that moment.

Oleh quipped: "I heard that the painting with the apostle Peter was taken to the Crimea, for some officer there, and the one with the pierced hands and feet got thrown into the dump." He sighed heavily. "So much for the advertised Russian spirituality and Christian roots!"

We left the office building. I decided to cautiously climb the concrete stairs to the second floor. It had been blown up. Wooden beams were scattered all over the area. I looked around, trying not to walk in my full height so as not to be seen by a sniper. Anywhere I turned on the campus, a whirlwind of memories rushed to my head, all from the peaceful times, when everything here at TCI was buzzing and breathing with life.

A blown-up car stood next to the ruined library. The letter Z stood out on its remains as an ominous swastika. I noticed books lying on the ground. It was as if someone had scattered them carelessly all over the area near the building. I bent down to pick up one of them. It was *Every Man a Warrior* by Lonnie Berger. I remembered that we had specially translated this three-volume Navigator series for men. Apparently, the title of the book looked repulsive to the Russian occupiers and gave them reason to believe that they were holding the very Nazi literature from which they had come to "liberate" us.

It was impossible to get into the library. There was such a layer of ash inside that feet would sink up to the ankle. No one could guarantee that there were no mines. I remembered how we had dreamed of having a library built, how carefully we had selected books to fill it, and now everything of value to us was burned inside, scattered around, or taken away by the occupiers.

We went toward the canteen. We had come across several boxes of Russian army rations scattered around the campus, as well as some sealed containers of rancid pickle soup. Not surprisingly, the Russian soldiers had looted all our food supplies for the students and kept looting the surrounding area. Locals told us that Russian officers forced them to grow tomatoes and potatoes for their needs.

The canteen building was all riddled with pockmarks after the mortar shelling. Inside, there were signs of looting. Beautiful paintings no longer hung on the walls as they used to. Tables and chairs, expensive kitchen equipment—everything was ripped out and taken away by the Russians. The same story with the toilets: there were no toilet brushes, no toilets, no sinks. Russians even stole ceiling lamps and wall sockets. In the women's restroom the only thing that survived was the sink. For some reason it could not be dismantled. Our laundry room had been equipped with industrial-grade washers and dryers; those were also stolen. The only thing left was a bizarre Russian warning on the wall: "Whoever does laundry and does not pay for the detergent, is a . . ." followed by an expletive. We can only guess what kind of atmosphere reigned among Russian soldiers, if they couldn't organize even their most mundane tasks properly, and apparently tried to cheat one another for a few pennies here and there, leaving alone the rampant looting they resorted to in the homes of those Ukrainians who left the occupied city.

We spend the most time examining the dorm in the Christmas Tree Building. In one of the rooms, we found a stack of black ribbons with Orthodox crosses and the inscription "Save and Keep Safe." I knew that such funeral ribbons were placed on the foreheads of the dead. This attribute was clearly left by Russian soldiers. The impression was that the priests blessed the Russian soldiers for the war and immediately gave them funeral ribbons—a blessing to die.

On the second floor of the Christmas Tree Building there were huge crimson bloodstains on the floor. What might have been going on there was anyone's guess. Perhaps it was used as a ward for the severely wounded or those who succumbed to their wounds. According to information from locals, which we cannot confirm independently, a Russian mobile crematorium was operating on the TCI campus. We were told that the Russians preferred to burn the corpses of their soldiers rather than bring them to the Crimea—an effort to avoid paying benefits to the relatives of soldiers killed in action. If this was true, it offers an explanation why this package of funeral ribbons was needed.

I had a great desire to walk along the embankment, but it was dangerous to go closer to the river beyond the middle alley, as that area was exposed to the opposite bank and could be monitored by Russian snipers. I could only approach the riverside in those spots where poplar trees provided sufficient concealment. In other areas I had to stay far enough away and look from afar, imagining how the Dnieper flowed behind the trees just as before. Indeed, the Dnieper has seen it all—the restless settlement of tribes along its course, some big wars and conflicts followed by reestablishment of peace, serene life, and here, in the winter of 2022, war breaking out again, and the area becoming the arena of new battles. Bridges collapsed. Machinery got blown up. People died.

I looked around. The once well-kept embankment looked abandoned and overgrown with weeds. Hundreds of shell casings were lying underfoot. I picked up one of them for the TCI museum. Stas came up to me. He noticed an abandoned kayak in the reeds. I remembered that we bought some expensive sports equipment for our students. Once again, I felt a surge of sadness: now it was all gone—the Russians had taken it all away. I restrained myself from taking a step to go and carefully pull the abandoned kayak ashore. It was probably booby-trapped. Russians do this on purpose to attract attention of kids, among others, so that more people could get blown up by mines. Insidious things like this make you shudder in horror as you realize they are done by those who have lived next to your land for centuries and liked to call your country a "fraternal nation."

For a moment, I thought that I had never felt such a dense and overhanging silence over an empty campus as I did on this November day. Since the time this plot of land had been acquired for the institute's infrastructure in 2005, I don't remember this place looking so empty and quiet. There have always been many people here: over there, in the shade of the trees, pastors liked to stroll; here, students spent their free time socializing and making new friends.

Now everything looked bleak, abandoned, and deserted. The wind touched the remaining leaves, and one could hear the creaking of my friend Oleh Derkachenko's prosthesis or the cautious footsteps of Stas, Anatoly, and Ivan. I stood still, stared, and listened. It seemed that my every sensory organ sharpened to recognize the new reality—the war. It was definitely here. I could smell it. I saw its footprints. I could even detect its sounds, even though on that day the sounds of war were not the rumble of explosions and slashing gunshots, but rather the dead silence of the abandoned campus. In this oppressive, mournful silence, it seemed as if time itself had frozen. It seemed as if everyone who found himself there at that time was asked to leave that place, once abuzz with a kaleidoscope of events and flamboyant life, without a single sound.

It was getting dark. We had to leave immediately. At dusk the Russians could resume shelling. The curfew in Kherson started at 6 p.m. We had to get home in time.

Chapter 29

Home

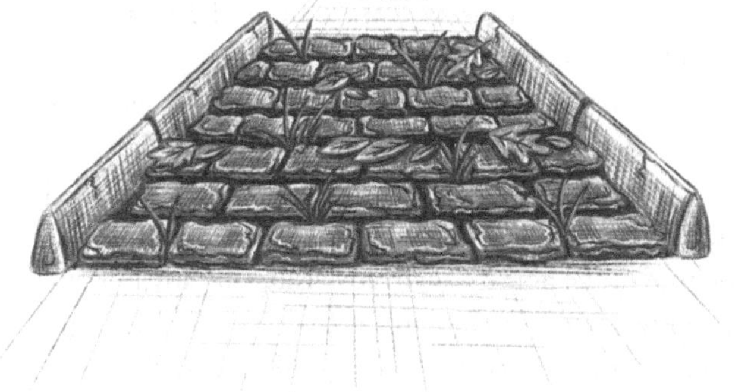

THE THOUGHT OF GOING HOME brought back a whirlwind of memories. They became even brighter as our gray Volkswagen Crafter approached the familiar neighborhood. I felt a lingering sense of anticipation building up. My emotions were like a roller coaster; my mood would rise and fall, and I would drift into melancholic memories.

Why am I being so moody? On the face of it, it seems like it was quite an ordinary thing: visit our home, get some things we needed, see our neighbors, give them some gifts. What's so special about it? Why do I care about it so much?

The roof of the house was already visible in early November twilight, and my eyes were looking at every curve. As we got closer, the brown-colored gate became more and more visible, and my eyes greedily absorbed the details that had become fuzzy in the last nine months but remained so dear to me.

I got out of the warm van and came up to the gate of my sweet home. My palm felt the coldness of the lock handle. I turned it, but the mechanism did not yield. The fresh autumn frost had enough bite to seize it, and it took a couple more tries to open it. Maybe this hiccup was for the best—the lock resistance didn't last long, not even a couple of minutes, but it brought me an unexpected smile: I knew about this feature of my gate, and it reminded me that I was finally home! I stepped into the yard.

My brother Stas was busy with the lock, trying to cycle it back and forth to make it work more smoothly. I looked around. The memories that had arisen in me a second ago were suddenly chilled.

Yes, this is my street; that's the spot where my family traditionally launch fireworks with our neighbors and congratulate each other on

New Year's Eve. This is my yard. Even the street Christmas garland, forgotten since last winter, is still there, all faded in the scorching southern sun—all of this is just like it was in my memories. But why does the courtyard seem so repulsively empty to me?

I realize that I am home. I try to be happy with these dried weeds, which in the absence of caring hands have grown and even raised some tiles here and there, and this is our small fir tree, growing lonely in the yard, and the juniper, about which I often joked that if I get depressed, like the prophet Elijah,* I will seek respite in its shadow—all of these details I remember so well.

But why can't I escape the feeling of emptiness? Maybe it's because the events of that February morning, when the whole family hurried to get away from the impending disaster, have come back to haunt me as well.

I heard Stas behind me. He was done with the lock and asked me not to take too long in the house. He had decided to go to visit our neighbors himself, to give them something from the humanitarian supplies he'd brought. His request brought me down to reality and reminded me that I had to hurry. I remembered all those hasty farewells exchanged with my brother Oleksandr when he decided to leave Ivano-Frankivsk, and the farewell to Maryna, Luba's sister, at the Polish border, and seeing my father this morning, when we couldn't finish our conversation. And here I am back home, something I've been craving for such a long time, and yet this visit also needs to be cut short.

The key turned in the lock with a familiar click. I stepped over the threshold and didn't expect to breathe in that cold air. I don't know why I expected to be greeted by the warmth of life, spiced with the aroma of the kitchen. No one had cooked here for nine long months; no one had gathered around the table for breakfast and dinner.

I found that the house was not only cold but also dark. The dim light barely penetrated from the street to the first floor—the pergola

* The story of the prophet Elijah from 1 Kings 19:4.

above the windows blocked it almost entirely. My hand reached for the light switch on the wall, out of habit. There was no power. I remembered that the city was almost all blacked out after the Russians left, including our neighborhood. I pulled out a small flashlight I had prepared in advance. Now, wherever its light fell, I saw a familiar home environment. I walked into the kitchen. It was drowning in darkness. All the chairs were pushed up to the dining table except for mine, which was pulled out as if inviting me to sit down. Everything was just as we left it when my family had eaten breakfast here for the last time—in the morning of February 24. The feeling of emptiness overpowered me again.

The flashlight beam hit a picture on the wall. My gaze lingered on it for a few moments. It was a memorable gift from my American friend Larry Cohn. He is a talented photographer. One day, when he visited with us here, Larry snapped a photo of a cherry tree he particularly liked in our garden. He then processed it so that everything was black and white except for one bright red cherry. It's been ten years since the tree no longer was there, but Larry's photo continues to remind me of it.

Familiar objects glinted in the darkness as I pointed the flashlight at them. Here is my collection of spoons from thirty countries. I've collected them meticulously. Those are bottles of Caucasian wine, given to me by ministers in the Republic of Georgia (part of their hospitable culture). It is noteworthy that none of the collections aroused any special feelings in me. It seemed as if they had completely lost their sentimental value to me. Maybe because it was more important for me to take the things my wife and daughter had asked me to bring back? I turned around to climb upstairs.

The steps of the wooden staircase leading upstairs creaked under the weight of my steps. My footsteps echoed lightly in the empty hallway. I went into the rooms one by one. I saw the evening sky and the first stars twinkling through the windows, but all neighboring houses were completely dark. I remembered how the lights of the street used to look. Now Kherson lay in darkness. Many houses, like ours, were empty. I looked around the children's bedrooms. I noticed how still their made beds stood. I saw the silent paintings on the walls and the silent books on the shelves. The frozen statuettes told me nothing. Everything was in its place, everything remained as it was before February, but the life itself was gone.

I lingered in Sonia's room. I remembered how she'd grown up. I shone the light on the map on the wall. It came alive with memories. Every time we traveled to a new country and came back, we erased it with a coin on the map, marking our visit. How many more places on Earth were to be discovered and mapped. But then it occurred to me that Sonia would probably never come back here. Her bachelorette party took place elsewhere. We had to do it away from home, in a rented apartment.

Chagrin pricked me like a needle. I thought fondly of the many bright family events that had taken place here at my house, and then I thought of all those that might take place here but never would. For a moment I felt robbed by the war—it was because of it that I was deprived of this happy place forever. The war took its toll on my children's happiness as well. They were also robbed. Of course, the house was still standing. No one touched it. But the war destroyed my life and the memories that connected my family with this place.

How much does it cost to re-create the homey atmosphere that used to be there?

What price tag do you put on an album of treasured family photos?

How would one quantify each little dash on the kitchen doorway that my wife and I had made as our kids grew?

I walked silently from one room to another with a sense of loss and emptiness. I felt indifference wherever I looked, whatever thing I touched, whatever the light of the flashlight fell on: bookshelves, clothes, furniture, household appliances—everything was no longer meaningful to me. It's such a strange realization: nothing that I had accumulated over my long forty-six years had any emotional response in me now. Everything that filled the house was sitting in the rooms, the attic, the basement, and the garage—everything lost its value at once. I realized that it used to be important and necessary. But I also realized that we had lived the last nine months without it all. I'm sure we'll do just fine without it for another nine months, or even nine years. Perhaps I felt that way because my family no longer lived here. We were no longer connected to this house.

I had to hurry to finish everything I needed to do before curfew. I grabbed things on my way as I walked around the house: my daughter's warm clothes, her favorite books, my wife's jacket, my winter shoes, my son's personal belongings. I wasn't even quite sure that I was picking up exactly what my family had asked me for. I headed for the door and was still struggling to come to terms with the realization that the life had been taken out of the house. I had come here with the desire to experience my prewar home that was alive in my memory, only to find a cold, lifeless shell that stood empty for nine months. There was no longer a single trace of its former coziness and warmth.

I stepped outside. Time was running out. The evening had already pushed deep shadows onto the town. The frosty air smelled with the freshness of the steppe. It was one of those things I sometimes missed in the west. There is something light, peaceful, and free in it—the smell of home! I realized that it was not going to be the only thing I would miss when I returned to Ivano-Frankivsk. I heard the distant rumble of explosions from the left bank of the Dnieper River—somewhere out there the battles raged on. Somewhere out there, the war was robbing other people, just as it robbed me.

Epilogue

The past is a foreign country.

—L. P. Hartley

THE IGNITION TURNED—my brother started the van. The headlights caught a few meters of the deserted street. Before slamming the gate shut, I looked around the yard for a farewell. My brother Oleksandr lived here. Now he and his family are far away. I will never hear the laughter of his children in this yard.

I felt the approach of winter in the air. It won't catch me here. Christmas and New Year's are just a month away, but I know for sure that I will not celebrate these holidays here. I have already celebrated Easter and my birthday away from here. My whole life is not here now.

I took one last look at the house. Before the war it was a happy place. Now I live in a rented apartment. The house, where a tight, loving family once lived and diligently worked to build simple human happiness, is empty. Perhaps for good. The war cut it off from its roots and stole its soul.

Acknowledgments

I AM IMMENSELY GRATEFUL to Yevhen Panov and Iryna Matvienko, my friends and editors of this book in Ukrainian and Russian, for their invaluable contribution in bringing it to life.

I deeply appreciate Maryna Polegenko, an artist from Kherson, who, like me, found herself displaced from her hometown yet still created the illustrations for this book.

My heartfelt gratitude goes to my wife, Luba, and my children, for their unwavering support throughout the writing process.

I am also grateful to the Board of Trustees of TCI and dear friends who provided great encouragement and became the first sponsors of this project in both Russian and Ukrainian.

I am sincerely grateful to Eurasia Mission for funding the publication of this book in Ukrainian and Russian.

Special thanks to my friends Volodymyr Stepanov and Yulia Lubinets, who assisted in translating this book into English, and to Mary Raber for her meticulous Russian-English editing.

Lastly, I am profoundly grateful to the Eerdmans team for taking the risk of publishing a book by an unknown author.

If the message of this book has moved you to financially help TCI rebuild its campus, you can give by visiting https://tavriskichristianinstitute.breezechms.com/give/online or by using this QR code.

Be sure to choose "give to campus replacement fund" in the dropdown menu.

If you would prefer to give by check, make the check out to TCI, and put "campus replacement" in the memo.

Send the check to:

TCI Foundation
6821 Willoughby Ct.
Indianapolis, IN 46214